CUBA
AFTER CASTRO
Legacies, Challenges, and Impediments

Edward Gonzalez, Kevin F. McCarthy

Prepared for the National Defense Research Institute

Approved for public release, distribution unlimited

RAND
CORPORATION

The research described in this report was sponsored by the RAND Corporation using its own funds.

Library of Congress Cataloging-in-Publication Data

Gonzalez, Edward.
    Cuba after Castro : legacies, challenges, and impediments / Edward Gonzalez, Kevin F. McCarthy.
      p. cm.
    "MG-111."
    Includes bibliographical references.
    ISBN 0-8330-3535-5 (pbk. : alk. paper)
    1. Cuba—Politics and government—1959– 2. Cuba—Social conditions—1959–
3. Social problems—Cuba—History—20th century. 4. Cuba—Economic
conditions—1990– 5. Cuba—Forecasting. 6. Economic forecasting—Cuba.
I. McCarthy, Kevin F., 1945– II.Title.

F1788.G58823 2004
320'.097291—dc22

                                           2004000924

The RAND Corporation is a nonprofit research organization providing objective analysis and effective solutions that address the challenges facing the public and private sectors around the world. RAND's publications do not necessarily reflect the opinions of its research clients and sponsors.

RAND® is a registered trademark.

Published 2004 by the RAND Corporation
1700 Main Street, P.O. Box 2138, Santa Monica, CA 90407-2138
1200 South Hayes Street, Arlington, VA 22202-5050
201 North Craig Street, Suite 202, Pittsburgh, PA 15213-1516
RAND URL: http://www.rand.org/
To order RAND documents or to obtain additional information, contact
Distribution Services: Telephone: (310) 451-7002;
Fax: (310) 451-6915; Email: order@rand.org

Preface

Cuba is nearing the end of the Castro era. When that end arrives, the government that succeeds Fidel Castro—as well as the Cuban people themselves—will arrive at a decisive crossroads in the island's tumultuous history. They will need answers to the following questions: How is the legacy of Castro's 44-plus-year rule likely to affect Cuba after Castro is gone? What are the political, social, and economic challenges that a post-Castro Cuba will have to confront? What are the impediments that will need to be surmounted if Cuba is to develop economically and embark upon a democratic transition?

To help address these and other questions, this report draws on the expertise of analysts both within and outside the RAND Corporation. Edward Gonzalez, Professor Emeritus at UCLA and a member of the Adjunct Staff at RAND, and Kevin McCarthy, Senior Social Scientist at RAND, are the report's principal investigators and co-authors. Besides writing this report, they are responsible for the political and demographic studies, respectively, which are part of a companion RAND report, *Cuba After Castro: Legacies, Challenges, and Impediments: Appendices,* TR-131-RC, 2004. Damián J. Fernández, Professor of International Relations at Florida International University, wrote the study on youth that appears in the companion Appendices volume. Dr. Jorge F. Pérez-López, a labor economist who has written extensively on the Cuban economy, wrote the studies on the island's economy and sugar industry that also appear in the companion report. (Although it informs this report, a sixth study commissioned by RAND, which is on race issues in Cuba, does not appear in the Appendices volume, but it is available from its author, Mark Q. Sawyer, Assistant Professor of Political Science at UCLA.) The analyses and findings of the five individual studies that are presented in the Appendices volume were then integrated by the co-authors into this report. This report should be of interest to U.S. policymakers and analysts concerned with Cuba, members of Congress, and a wider audience outside the U.S. government.

This report and the companion volume build on a long tradition of RAND research on Cuba. Among the most relevant studies are the following:

- Edward Gonzalez and David F. Ronfeldt, *Cuba Adrift in a Post-communist World*, R-4231-USDP, 1992
- Edward Gonzalez and David F. Ronfeldt, *Storm Warnings for Cuba*, MR-452-OSD, 1994
- Edward Gonzalez, *Cuba: Clearing Perilous Waters?* MR-673-OSD, 1996.

This report results from RAND's continuing program of self-sponsored independent research. Support for such research is provided, in part, by donors and by the independent research and development provisions of RAND's contracts for the operation of its U.S. Department of Defense federally funded research and development centers.

This research was overseen by the RAND National Security Research Division (NSRD), a division of the RAND Corporation. NSRD conducts research and analysis for the Office of the Secretary of Defense, the Joint Staff, the unified commands, the defense agencies, the Department of the Navy, the U.S. intelligence community, allied foreign governments, and foundations.

The RAND Corporation Quality Assurance Process

Peer review is an integral part of all RAND research projects. Prior to publication, this document, as with all documents in the RAND monograph series, was subject to a quality assurance process to ensure that the research meets several standards, including the following: The problem is well formulated; the research approach is well designed and well executed; the data and assumptions are sound; the findings are useful and advance knowledge; the implications and recommendations follow logically from the findings and are explained thoroughly; the documentation is accurate, understandable, cogent, and temperate in tone; the research demonstrates understanding of related previous studies; and the research is relevant, objective, independent, and balanced. Peer review is conducted by research professionals who were not members of the project team.

RAND routinely reviews and refines its quality assurance process and also conducts periodic external and internal reviews of the quality of its body of work. For additional details regarding the RAND quality assurance process, visit http://www.rand.org/standards/.

Contents

Executive Summary

Cuba's economy is in trouble. Social tensions are rising. Fidel Castro is aging. Now 77 (as of this writing), the end is thus looming for the linchpin who has held the political system together for more than 44 years. Once this *caudillo,* or strongman, departs, his successors will be saddled with a weak state, along with daunting political, economic, and demographic problems—in short, a vast array of dysfunctional legacies from the *fidelista* past.

A post-Castro regime that tries to remain communist may soon find itself in a cul-de-sac where old policies and instruments no longer work. If or when such a regime falters, there is a remote possibility that a democracy-oriented government could replace it. But Cuba's civil-society and market actors look too embryonic, and democratic political opposition forces too decimated, for a pro-democracy upheaval to take hold naturally. A more likely scenario is that the military, arguably Cuba's most important institution, will take control of the government (perhaps much as General Wojciech Jaruzelski did in Poland from 1981 to 1989).

Cuba's Weakening, Distorted State

The conditions that enabled the Castro regime to function well for so many decades have deteriorated sharply since 1989. Three of the four pillars—Soviet support, the Revolution, and the totalitarian state apparatus—that long sustained the regime have collapsed or weakened. The fourth—Fidel Castro himself—will cease to exist with the *caudillo*'s passing, leaving his successors to face a far more precarious future than what would have been the case 15 or 20 years ago.

The Regime's Eroding Pillars of Support

The first pillar to give way was the Soviet Union. The economic support that contributed 21 percent to Cuba's gross national product (GNP) in the 1980s disappeared after 1991 following the collapse of the Soviet Union, and the island's GDP soon plummeted by one-third. Although the economic free fall was subsequently checked, growth rates fell in 2002 and 2003, with the 2003 sugar harvest being the worst harvest in 70 years. The result is that Cubans no longer can expect to regain their 1989 living standards by 2009, as was once the case.

The loss of Soviet (and Council of Mutual Economic Assistance [CMEA]) trade, aid, and subsidies undermined a second pillar: the "Revolution" and the social compact it represented for ordinary Cubans. Soviet largesse had enabled the Cuban government to provide citizens with an array of free or subsidized goods and benefits, which helped maintain Cubans' allegiance. But following the demise of Soviet assistance, Havana had to enact a "Special Period" of heightened austerity, a period that started in 1990 and continues to this day. The oft-heralded system of free health care deteriorated badly as basic medicines became unavailable. Employment in the state sector had to be cut. Subsidized monthly food rations were slashed to ten days' worth, and shortages in consumer goods spread—all of which forced Cubans to turn increasingly to the black market and other illicit activities in order to "*resolver*" (make do). Meanwhile, income inequalities grew exponentially between those with pesos, who were losing their purchasing power, and those with dollars. And even those Cubans with dollars found themselves barred from stores, restaurants, hotels, and resorts reserved exclusively for tourists. Hence, as popular disillusionment has deepened, Cuba's "failed revolution" is unlikely to provide Castro's heirs with a legitimizing mystique.

The regime's third pillar, the totalitarian state apparatus, had been in place since the 1960s. It had long enabled the regime to penetrate, control, and mobilize the population until the collapse of the Soviet pillar undermined its power and reach. It then mutated into a less penetrative, less controlling post-totalitarian state, which had to cede some economic and social—but not political—space to society in the early 1990s. A small private sector was thus legalized so that consumer shortages and unemployment could be eased. The Roman Catholic Church, Protestant denominations, and Afro-Cuban sects became more active. Political dissidents, human-rights activists, and independent journalists and librarians came forward, challenging the regime's grip on all power and information. And in 2002, the Varela Project collected more than 11,000 signatures for a petition calling for political and economic reforms. Faced with these challenges, and wary of the growing prospects of unrest, the regime rounded up and imprisoned 75 dissidents and independent journalists and librarians in spring 2003, which decimated the opposition and emerging civil-society actors. But if Castro's successors try to compensate for the state's weakness by continuing to use open, heavy-handed repression, they will further risk delegitimizing the new regime.

The fourth and final pillar of support has been Fidel Castro himself. Despite age, illness, and growing irascibility, the *líder máximo* still casts an aura of legitimacy over Cuba's government, state, and Party institutions. He also gives the regime a sense of direction and cohesion. His passing will leave a leadership void that is unlikely to be filled by his designated successor, Raúl Castro, or by any other government or Communist Party leader. Regime divisions are certain to erupt in the absence of *el comandante.*

Dysfunctional Political Legacies

A post-Castro government, whether communist or noncommunist, will find itself burdened by two troublesome legacies from the Castro era: caudilloism, and totalitarianism/post-totalitarianism. The first legacy will hobble the new government; the second legacy will leave society deformed.

The culture of caudilloism (rule by a strongman) will exacerbate the sense of a leadership void and hamper a new regime's ability to govern and embark on policy shifts. Rule by Castro led to the stunting of autonomous institutions after 1959, serving to ensure his own power and that of his brother and other ruling elites. In addition, Castro pursued populist policies that a successor government may find difficult to deviate from, even if they are known to be not in Cuba's best interest. A case in point is Castro's ultra-defiant posture toward the United States; continuation of that posture by a new government is certain to deprive Cuba of needed economic and technical assistance. Another is Castro's pursuit of a "moral" economy—essentially an egalitarian, classless, nonmaterialist, socialist system. This stance has kept him from accepting market-type reforms, and it may limit a successor government's ability to change course for fear of a *fidelista* backlash.

The legacy of totalitarianism/post-totalitarianism will leave post-Castro Cuba without the rule of law and other legal requisites that can help restrain the power of the state, promote a market-based economy, and enable civil-society organizations to act vigorously in support of a democratic transition. This legacy is bound to exacerbate polarization between committed *fidelistas* and those "outside the Revolution" who have suffered directly from not only state repression but also betrayal and condemnation by their neighbors, fellow workers, and even family members.

Pervasive societal mistrust and politicization have left a growing number of Cubans, both old and young, politically exhausted, disenchanted, and disengaged. This condition does not bode a smooth democratic transition or even continuance of post-totalitarianism, because sectors of the population already are resisting the kinds of mass mobilizations that were once routine during the Castro era.

A People at Odds: Generational, Racial, and Demographic Divisions

The specter of a people united by Castro and the Revolution conceals a different social reality. Cuban society exhibits three major and potentially divisive cleavages that involve youth, race, and an aging population.

An Alienated Youth

Following a common pattern in Cuban history, the Revolution was made by a new leadership generation: Fidel Castro was 32 years old when he seized power; his brother and others in the victorious Rebel Army were younger still. Almost at once, the new government set out to ensure the permanency of the Revolution by creating, in Castro's words, "a more perfect generation" among the young. To this end, it employed education, the mass media, and membership in the Young Pioneers and the Union of Young Communists, aiming to mold Cuban youth (the 16-to-30-year-old age group) in the image of Che Guevara's "new communist man."

However, relations between the state and Cuba's youth began to deteriorate in the late 1970s, when exiles returning to the island gave young Cubans a new view of life in the United States. Further strains developed in the 1980s, when, contrary to Castro's anti-liberalization stance, the advent of *glasnost* and *perestroika* in the Soviet Union garnered enthusiastic support among Cuban youth. Tensions intensified after 1989, when the young faced heightened austerity, few opportunities for upward mobility, and unfulfilled aspirations—not only material, but also creative and spiritual. As a result, more and more youths turned away from official dogma and prescribed norms and began embracing Western pop music and other fads, dropping out, hustling, and engaging in prostitution. Cuban youth became increasingly disaffected and disconnected from politics as the 1990s wore on.

The regime tried to win back their support by, among other things, giving young "loyalists" positions in the Party, in state and military structures, and in enterprises in the new-dollar sectors of the economy. Although the bulk of Cuban youth remain disaffected, they have split into two remaining camps. On the one hand, the "in-betweens" are alienated because their personal expectations have been dashed, but they might still support a socialist state if it provides greater personal freedom and authentic political participation than the current regime. The "opponents," on the other hand, reject socialism, attend religious services, adopt Western mores, and are generally more self-absorbed. The challenge facing the present regime—and a successor—is to win over the "in-between" group or at least prevent it from moving into the opposition camp, both of which actions may become impossible to achieve if heightened repression continues and the economy worsens.

The retreat from politics among Cuban youth may pose problems for not only a successor communist regime but also a democratically oriented one, because each would lack support from this pivotal, alienated sector of the population. Democratic institutions, norms, and practices cannot take root without active acceptance and participation. Mass emigration by disaffected young, in turn, could prove devastating to the island's future economic prospects.

A Growing Racial Divide

Castro's government made great strides in promoting racial equality after 1959. Afro-Cubans benefited from the outlawing of overt racial discrimination and from the government's commitment to improving the lot of the poor, a disproportionate percentage of whom were blacks and mulattos. When white middle-class flight opened up job opportunities and housing stock for blacks and mulattos in the 1960s, Afro-Cubans became the most enthusiastic supporters of the new regime and of the persona of "Fidel" in particular.

Despite Afro-Cubans' obtaining near-equality with whites in terms of longevity, education, and occupation, many racial inequalities persisted in the 1980s. Blacks and mulattos make up nearly half the population, but they continue to represent a disproportionate share of the prison population, and they still live in the most dilapidated areas of Havana and other cities. Blacks and mulattos remain heavily concentrated in the poorest, easternmost provinces, which formerly formed the province of Oriente.

In the 1990s, racial inequality and discrimination rose sharply during the Special Period. While most Cubans suffered from the Special Period's austerity, the plight of Afro-Cubans—especially blacks—was made even worse by the dollarization of the economy in 1993, which has divided society into those with access to dollars and those without access to dollars. Afro-Cubans find themselves in the latter camp. For one thing, they receive far fewer dollar remittances from the mostly white Cuban-American exile community. Second, they are less likely to be small peasant farmers, who can sell surplus produce for dollars in the farmers' markets. Third, they (particularly blacks) have been largely excluded from employment in the tourist sector due to discrimination. Internal migration from the less-developed eastern provinces by so-called darker-skinned *palestinos* has also been blamed for rising crime rates in Havana, which has increased racial tensions and prompted Afro-Cubans to complain of discrimination and police harassment. In the meantime, blacks and mulattos remain quite underrepresented in the leadership ranks of the regime's key institutions.

Such racial issues spell trouble for any future government in Cuba. Not even a successor communist regime may be able to attract the fervent support that Afro-Cubans once offered to the Castro regime, and to Fidel above all. Any type of post-Castro government will have to better the lot of Afro-Cubans substantially if it is to win their support. But a new government, communist or not, will likely find its policy options for expanding the economy constrained because so many Afro-Cubans, along with other skeptical sectors of the population, may oppose liberal economic reforms and increased foreign investments as a result of their already-negative experiences with the new economy. Meanwhile, a new government will need to develop the eastern half of the island if it is to improve employment for Afro-Cubans and stem internal migration. However, such a development will require allocating scarce resources away from other regions and constituencies, a move that could intensify Cuba's looming racial and regional divide.

In short, race is likely to compound divisiveness in the new Cuba because it overlaps and reinforces other divisions between Afro-Cubans and whites. Race is a factor in Cubans' religious affiliation (*Santería* and other syncretic Afro-Cuban sects versus Catholicism and Protestantism), preferences for the economic system (socialist versus market-driven), and competing notions about political power (race-based representation, versus continued white control of the government).

An Aging Population

Cuba's prospects for economic recovery and sustained growth will be further hampered by its overall demographic structure, which resembles that of a developed country more than the demographic structures of its Caribbean and Latin American neighbors. Cuba's population has been growing at less than 1.0 percent per year since 1980, with an even slower growth (0.2 percent) projected for the 2003–2025 period. Its aged population (65 years and older) will become the most rapidly growing segment over the next two decades. As its population grows older, the size of younger cohorts entering the workforce will decrease.

As a consequence of these demographic changes, demand for social services for the older population—retirement pensions, health care, etc.—will increase at the very time that the working population needed to support such services will itself be aging and decreasing. This demographic conundrum will be compounded by the depressed state of the economy, because Cuba will lack the financial resources to continue providing early retirement with a state pension for its elderly, starting at age 55 for women and 60 for men.

Hence, any new government will face difficult public policy choices with respect to (a) supporting Cuba's aging population, (b) allocating scarce resources among competing social programs, and (c) developing a labor force to pay for future increases in social expenditures. Finding solutions to these problems will entail political risks that a future, presumably weaker, government may prefer to avoid and that, in any case, may be unrealistic in the Cuban context. Details of each problem are discussed briefly below.

Revising the pension system by raising the retirement age, for example, is likely to produce a sharp reaction from future retirees. Requiring workers to contribute to their own retirement could also provoke strong opposition from younger workers, especially if the real value of their wages remains low and the economy depressed. Moreover, shifting pension responsibility from the state to private employers hardly seems feasible in the Cuban context, because the state has played the overwhelmingly dominant role in the economy and social sector for the past 44-plus years. Even if a market-based system were adopted, saddling the nascent private sector with paying for pensions would place an enormous burden on it.

A new government will have to decide how much of Cuba's gross domestic product (GDP) should be devoted to social services and how to allocate that amount between the young and the old. Reducing current consumption levels, including those for social services, in order to invest in future growth should, in theory, yield higher incomes and resources for future consumption. But such a cutback would be painful, if not impossible, given the island's low levels of income and economic development. However, devoting a larger share of GDP to social services would increase the burden on workers who have already absorbed cutbacks in real wages and would further increase political disaffection among the young.

As to allocating social spending between the young and the old, a new government will find it difficult to find the resources to satisfy both sectors. An expected decline in the school-age population should result in a decline in total government expenditures for the young, especially for education. But that reduction will surely be insufficient to fund a significant increase in expenditures for Cuba's aging population. It may make more sense to allocate greater resources to improving education, particularly at the university level, given Cuba's critical need for economic growth and global competitiveness.[1]

Finally, post-Castro Cuba will face not only a shortage of capital and natural resources, but also a shrinking labor pool. To expand the size of its workforce, it could raise retirement ages and/or increase labor force participation among prime-age workers. However, both options would require major departures from the policies of the Castro era: Wages would have to be tied to productivity, thereby reversing the Revolution's commitment to reducing income inequalities.

---

[1] We recognize that increasing the resources Cuba devotes to its higher education system runs counter to World Bank and Inter-American Development Bank (IDB) experience in the less-developed countries, where investment in basic skills appears to have a higher development payoff. However, we believe that our approach is better suited to Cuba's economic situation. Cubans' basic educational levels are already high by most developing-country standards, and Cuba's long-term economic growth will likely hinge on the availability of highly skilled and professional labor.

Moreover, an emphasis would have to be placed on promoting economic efficiency, thereby reversing the Revolution's old commitment to full employment. Thus far, the Castro regime has refused to take either step. Whether a weaker, successor government can reverse course remains to be seen.

Cuba's Ever-Failing Economy

Cuba's economy, never in good shape, is now approaching a critical juncture. To stem the economic free fall after 1989, the Castro government opened the economy to foreign investors and rebuilt the tourist industry in order to recapture hard currency. For a while, these and other modest reforms helped stop the hemorrhaging, but by 2002 new signs indicated that the economy was slowing again.

Indeed, unless Castro defies all expectations by further altering course, he will displace onto his heirs the task of making the systemic changes Cuba needs before it can achieve the sustained economic growth that can help legitimize a post-Castro government. It will thus be left to a new government to raise labor productivity and stem corruption in both the state and society. And the new government will be faced with the equally formidable tasks of overturning the command economy, ceding a measure of control to a revitalized private sector, and transforming the island's distorted industrial structure.

An Unproductive Labor Force

Among the key factors affecting the prospects for revitalizing the economy is Cuba's highly educated but low-productivity labor force. The low productivity has been exacerbated by the declining state of Cuba's capital stock, its shortage of investment capital, and its lack of raw materials. But the Castro regime's policies regarding full employment and wages have also played a role. The commitment to full employment transformed open unemployment into rampant underemployment prior to 1989, when Soviet economic support was available, and then worsened it during the Special Period, when the economy was at its lowest ebb. Thus, despite the closure of 45 percent of the island's most inefficient sugar mills in 2002, the Castro regime has kept the displaced workers on the state payroll. Setting wages according to a national pay schedule has further compounded the problem of low productivity by divorcing workers' wages from their productivity—a policy that has motivated poor work habits and created disincentives for maximizing production among the labor force. The new regime will thus be faced with a long-term task of motivating workers anew through market incentives.

A Repressed and Deformed Private Sector

Another impediment is the weakness of the small, deformed private sector that will be left from the Castro era. The regime has resisted the development of a healthy private sector, mainly because of Fidel's ideological commitment to socialism and his obsession with his place in history, but also because of other political calculations. His regime is determined to prevent the rise of a middle class that may challenge its power, and to constrain the growth of income equalities that may undermine regime support among state employees, Party workers, military and security personnel, and pensioners, many of whom must subsist on peso-denominated incomes.

Bowing to necessity in 1993, the regime legalized self-employment in micro-enterprises to generate trades, crafts, and services that the state was no longer able to supply and to provide new employment opportunities. By 1997, the number of micro-enterprises had grown to more than 200,000. But when the economy showed signs of recovery, and the self-employed showed that they were enjoying substantial dollar incomes, the regime actively discouraged further growth of the fledgling private sector by erecting new obstacles. By 2001, the number of micro-enterprises dropped to an estimated 150,000. In addition, the private sector has become increasingly deformed. The absence of a private distribution system has led to the widespread pilfering of state stores and to the buying of stolen supplies on the black market. Moreover, as a result of 40-plus years of communism, the labor force lacks the kinds of trained managers, accountants, auditors, bankers, insurers, etc., that a robust market economy requires.

A Corrupt Society and State

Yet another obstacle to revitalizing the economy is the prevalence of corruption and favoritism. Most materials on the black market are stolen or misappropriated from state enterprises and warehouses. Inside deals are commonplace between individuals and their government contacts. Privileges are accorded to the *nomenklatura* (known in Cuba as *pinchos grandes*). And the government selectively privatizes state enterprises and creates new joint enterprises for the benefit of trusted civilian and military loyalists assigned to run them.

A Postponed Imperative: Restructuring the Economy

If it wants to promote the island's integration into the global economy, a new government will also have to transform the distorted industrial structure that developed as a result of Cuba's close economic ties to the Soviet Union. The intertwining of the Cuban economy with that of the U.S.S.R. not only insulated it from the international market but also distorted it as a result of the extremely high prices the Soviets paid for Cuban sugar exports and the low prices that Cuba paid for Soviet oil imports (which Cuba could re-export to the world market) and for other raw-material and industrial inputs. As a result, the Castro government long concentrated its resources on increasing sugar production, which reached levels of 7 to 8 million metric tons in the 1980s, at the expense of diversifying the rest of agricultural and non-agrarian sectors of the economy. The sugar industry itself became distorted under the artificially favorable conditions it enjoyed as inefficient sugar mills and unproductive sugar fields were kept in operation.

Absent Soviet support, sugar production thus began to drop steadily beginning in 1992–1993. Moreover, the high cost of sugar production in Cuba limited its export options, because the cost of Cuban sugar exceeded the declining world-market price for sugar. Despite the restructuring of the industry that began in 2002, including the permanent closure of 71 of the most inefficient mills, production has now plummeted to a reported 2 million tons in 2003. A new government will therefore be faced with the difficult challenge of further scaling down the industry and introducing other efficiency measures—including laying off workers—to make it more competitive on the world market.

Additional economic distortions will have to be overcome, which will be no less daunting for the new government. Obsolete industrial plants and equipment, much of it acquired from the former Soviet Union and Eastern bloc, will have to be replaced. Domestic linkages, virtually non-existent at present, will need to be promoted in order to bolster the small private sector and ease the economy's heavy reliance on imported manufacturing inputs. If a market economy is to take hold and thrive, the rule of law, required to protect property rights and provide predictable and enforceable contract laws and a secure environment for investors, will have to be observed by both government officials and the public alike. These and other undertakings are likely to take years, possibly generations, to accomplish.

Policy Implications for the United States

The policies that the United States follows after Castro leaves the scene could have a major effect on whether Cuba remains under hard-line or reformist communist rule, falls under military governance, begins a democratic transition, or is gripped by instability and strife. To help foster a stable, prosperous, democratic Cuba, the United States should observe the following policy guidelines:

- Use the prospect of lifting the embargo (if still in effect) as leverage to move a successor communist regime toward a democratic transition. Lift the embargo if a democratically oriented regime comes to power.
- Work in concert with Canada and the United Kingdom, Spain, and other countries in the European Union in trying to influence events in a post-Castro Cuba along the lines of a democratic outcome.
- Avoid public postures that incite Cuban nationalism and work to the advantage of hard-liners. Cultivate informal military-to-

military contacts and use public diplomacy to make clear the United States' willingness to respect Cuba's independence, sovereignty, and dignity. But also make clear that Havana needs to reciprocate by respecting human rights and evolving toward a market-based democracy.

- Restore full diplomatic and trade relations once the Cuban government is committed to a democratic transition and offer economic and technical assistance to jump-start the economy.
- Encourage the private sector, the academy, nongovernment organizations (NGOs), and especially the Cuban-American community to become engaged and assist Cuba in embarking on a democratic transition.
- Offer to renegotiate the status of the Guantanamo Naval Base once the transition is under way.

Cuba will be at a critical crossroads when the Castro era comes to an end. Cuba could become a "failed state," in which case the United States would be faced with internal disorder and a humanitarian crisis on the island, and with uncontrolled drug flows and mass migration to the United States. Hence, the United States needs to offer the Cuban people a new deal along the above lines, with the aim of not only avoiding a worst-case scenario on the island but also helping Cuba to move toward a more stable, prosperous, and democratic outcome.

Acknowledgments

The authors wish to thank the two reviewers of the initial draft manuscript, Nurith Berstein and George Plinio Montalván, for their helpful criticisms, comments, and suggestions, which vastly improved the final report. Their contributions were rendered despite extremely tight time constraints, and their cooperation in meeting deadlines is most appreciated. David Ronfeldt needs to be singled out for his contribution in reworking the Executive Summary so that it became more arresting as well as more readable. Marian Branch and Nancy DelFavero contributed their editorial skills in ensuring that the report met RAND standards. In providing secretarial support, Lisa Lewis and Judy Rohloff maintained both steadiness and a sense of perspective as they were prevailed upon countless times to enter changes to the manuscript under conditions of mounting stress on the part of one of the harried authors. We also wish to acknowledge the diligent work of our research assistant Conner Spreng in rooting out articles and data in the early stages of our work. Finally, both authors wish to acknowledge the wise counsel that Rachel Swanger provided, from the project's conceptual stage to its final completion in fall 2003.

CHAPTER ONE

INTRODUCTION

Cuba is nearing the end of the Castro era. The government that succeeds Fidel Castro—as well as the Cuban people themselves—will arrive at a decisive crossroads in the island's tumultuous history. When that end arrives, they will need to answer a series of questions: How is the legacy of Castro's 44-plus-year rule likely to affect Cuba after Castro is gone? What are the political, social, and economic challenges that a post-Castro Cuba will likely confront? What are the structural impediments that will need to be surmounted if Cuba is to develop economically and embark on a democratic transition?

The analysis that follows addresses these issues. It synthesizes and integrates the findings of the research papers developed for this analysis, most of which appear in a companion RAND technical report (Gonzalez, Edward, and Kevin F. McCarthy, *Cuba After Castro: Legacies, Challenges, and Impediments: Appendices,* TR-131-RC, 2004).

This report addresses five major challenges. Part I covers the first three:

- The twin political legacies of caudilloism (rule by a strongman) and totalitarianism/post-totalitarianism that will burden the new government, whether it is a communist successor regime or a democratically oriented regime, and arrest the development of a law-based civil society.
- A growing number of alienated youth, whose disaffection is due both to nonfulfillment of their personal aspirations, especially

after 1989, and to the regime's failure to live up to its high-minded ideals. These youth, once viewed as the promise of the Revolution, will likely prove difficult to re-engage politically.

- A looming cleavage between white Cubans and Afro-Cubans, stemming not only from the growing racial discrimination of recent years but also from different expectations concerning the distribution of political power and economic wealth in a new Cuba.

Part II then focuses on two major structural problems:

- An emerging demographic bind, in which Cuba's population is rapidly aging at the same time that its shrinking supply of young workers will not be able to support either old-age entitlements or Cubans' educational, health, and other needs.
- An economic legacy of deformed institutions and an obsolete and inefficient sugar industry that has left Cuba ill prepared to make the needed transition into a global economy. Cuba's economy will require substantial restructuring along market-driven lines if it is to produce sustained economic growth and development required to meet the demands that will be placed on the new government.

The analysis in this report will show how these problems are interconnected and how, individually and in combination, they will pose very difficult policy choices for a new post-Castro government. Failure to meet these challenges is certain to further weaken the successor government's fragile legitimacy, thus lessening its capacity to marshal the public support needed for Cuba's political and economic reconstruction, including the long-term process of moving toward national reconciliation.

Part I:
Political Legacies, Social Challenges

Signs of political change and growing uncertainty abound in Cuba. In the spring of 2002, more than 11,000 Cubans dared sign their names to the Varela Project, in which they petitioned the National Assembly to enact liberalizing political and economic reforms. Less than a year later, on March 18, 2003, the Cuban government responded by rounding up 75 prominent dissidents, independent journalists, and librarians, and sentencing them to prison terms of six to 28 years. Three Afro-Cubans, meanwhile, were executed for attempting to hijack a boat in a vain attempt to flee the island. When international condemnation of these actions followed, Fidel Castro, Cuba's aging patriarch, in a sign of increasing irascibility, leveled bitter, vitriolic attacks against the European Union and the Spanish and Italian prime ministers. In the meantime, the Cuban economy is again faltering and the European Union has refused to sign a cooperation agreement with Cuba. Prospects are that social tensions could worsen in the months ahead. These developments, and the continuing delay in convening the Sixth Communist Party Congress, suggest that the Cuban leadership is both apprehensive and uncertain over what course changes it should make as the Castro era nears its end.

Indeed, the government that follows Castro will face daunting political, social, and economic challenges, including some that are of a structural nature that will require fundamental systemic changes if they are to be resolved. However, Cuba's future government, whether communist or non-communist, is certain to be constrained by the legacy of its past in trying to cope with the challenges ahead. A large part of this constraint is due to the *comandante*'s more than four decades of *caudillo*-like and totalitarian/post-totalitarian rule. The future government will further be haunted by the policies pursued by his regime, which, for the most part, either delayed or exacerbated the severity of the political, social, and economic problems that lie ahead.

Castro's successors may well find themselves in a dead end: Conditions once conducive to Cuba's maximalist state no longer exist, and the state-controlled economy will be unable to satisfy the long-suppressed demands of Cuban consumers and reinvigorate the government's various social programs. The state apparatus will be weakened by the absence of the Revolution's founder and charismatic leader just when the new government must cope with the problems of youth, race, an aging population, and a slowing economy. Indeed, if they are to be surmounted, these problems in themselves will require that the basic structure of the Cuban polity and economy be altered fundamentally and rapidly; otherwise, Cuba could find itself paralyzed by simultaneous, multiple crises.

CHAPTER TWO

Castro's Political Legacies: Caudilloism and Totalitarianism[1]

The analysis that follows has two overarching themes. One is that the pillars of support upon which the Castro regime has relied over the past decades have either collapsed or been seriously weakened. As a result, the communist government that will likely succeed Cuba's *líder máximo* is likely to find itself in a tenuous position. The other is that the *caudillo,* or strongman, and totalitarian/post-totalitarian legacies bequeathed by the Castro regime will greatly complicate governance on the part of the successor regime, whatever its character, and impair the emergence of a civil society that would be supportive of a post-Castro political system.

Background

After assuming full powers following his near-mythical triumph over the dictatorship of Fulgencio Batista in 1959, Fidel Castro would become Cuba's—and Latin America's—greatest and longest-reigning *caudillo.* But Castro is not the typical *caudillo.* Buttressed by Castro's charismatic appeal, a popular, redistributive revolution that benefited the lot of the Cuban people, and Soviet economic and military assistance, Cuba developed a powerful state apparatus in the post-Revolutionary period. Enjoying wide popular support even as it decimated civil society, Cuba's new revolutionary government

---

[1] This chapter is drawn from Edward Gonzalez (2004, Appendix A).

evolved into a single-party totalitarian state, starting in the mid-1960s: It was guided by a ruling ideology that fused *fidelismo* with a radicalized version of Marxism that aimed at transforming Cuban society. It eliminated pluralism as the private sector was replaced by an increasingly centralized command economy; at the same time, autonomous social institutions were taken over, dismantled, or cowed into submission. And through its state and Party organs, it penetrated deeply into society, providing the Castro regime with far greater control over individual citizens than traditional authoritarian regimes in the rest of Latin America had.

Cuba's powerful state apparatus not only enabled the Castro regime to repel U.S. aggression and ride out the potentially destabilizing effects of the more-than-four-decades-old U.S. embargo. It also enabled Castro to project Cuba's influence worldwide—including through the dispatch of combat troops to Africa in the 1970s and 1980s. Further, it enabled the regime to carry out a radical social revolution that extinguished most of the nonagrarian private sector, redistributed private property either on an individual basis or on a mostly collective basis, and eliminated the vestiges of Cuba's pre-1959 civil society.

The power and reach of Cuba's totalitarian state were greatly strengthened by the Castro government's close ties to Moscow. Begun in 1960 and, after surviving the strains caused by Nikita Khrushchev's withdrawal of Soviet missiles in the October 1962 crisis, these ties grew steadily to the point that Cuba became a privileged client-state of the Soviet Union. Soviet arms transformed Cuba's armed forces into Latin America's most potent, battle-tested military (Suchlicki, 1989). More important in terms of the regime's political survival at home, Soviet economic largesse enabled Cuba to overcome the effects of the U.S. economic embargo and, just as important, enabled the regime to deliver on the social compact between state and society: Cuban citizens were provided with an array of social goods—free health care and education, low-cost housing, subsidized food rations, and state employment—in exchange for their loyalty and support.

Pillars of Support for the Castro Regime, 1959–1991

Seen in retrospect, the Castro regime rested on four pillars of internal and external support during the first three decades of its existence.

The first was the great *caudillo* himself, Fidel Castro, who from the outset enjoyed enthusiastic personal support and loyalty from the majority of the populace when he seized power in 1959. Fidel's persona was immediately invested with charismatic authority as the young rebel chieftain who had miraculously delivered Cuba from the Batista dictatorship; in the eyes of his followers, he was now the chosen leader, destined to continue performing miracles on behalf of the fatherland. A gifted orator, he articulated the aspirations of the common man and effectively manipulated symbols of nationalism and anti-Americanism to rally popular support. Although his charisma would wane following the 1970 sugar harvest debacle, and although Cubans would become increasingly weary of the personal sacrifices and repression they had to endure, he would remain like China's Mao Tse-tung—Cuba's "Great Helmsman."

The second pillar of support was the "Revolution," which combined nationalistic defiance of the United States with popular, responsive government and a social compact between the state and its people. Under the social compact, the state promised to deliver a better life to its citizens in return for their support and devotion to the Revolution. Hence, the revolutionary government bettered the standard of living of the rural population, committed itself to a policy of full employment, and provided blacks and mulattos with equal access to government jobs, higher education, and the professions. In addition, extensive entitlements were given to all Cubans—from free health care and education, and low-priced rationed foodstuffs, to early retirement with a pension.

The third supportive pillar was the totalitarian state apparatus. Its erection greatly strengthened the regime's control over the population and rid society of pluralism. The movement toward totalitarianism had been under way since the sweeping nationalization decrees that began in 1960 eliminated large and medium-sized privately owned Cuban enterprises, as well as large and medium-sized private farms, which were also converted into collectives or state-farms under the Second Agrarian Reform Law of 1963. The state had taken over most autonomous civil-society institutions of the pre-1959 era—private schools, trade unions, and professional associations, for example—along with newspapers and radio and TV stations in the early 1960s. Although it remained independent of the state, the Catholic Church had been effectively neutered in the same period with the government's expulsion of priests and nuns, after which the Church would remain a compliant institution. In the meantime, Cuban society had become thoroughly penetrated and controlled through State Security and its agents and legions of spies and informers—ordinary citizens who, through conviction, loyalty, fear, malice, or self-interest, became accomplices of the totalitarian state

The totalitarian breakthrough came when Cuba formally became a one-party state, with the unveiling of the new Communist Party of Cuba (PCC) in 1965. *Fidelismo* was fused with radical Marxist thought as the regime's guiding ideology, the goal being to eradicate capitalism fully, construct "genuine communism," and create the "new communist man." What was left of the urban private sector—some 55,000 small shops, restaurants, barbershops, food stands, etc.—was swept away by the "Revolutionary Offensive" of 1968, thereby eliminating the last remnants of pluralism.

The boundaries of Cuba's totalitarian state thus became coterminous with those of society. State organs, principally through the Party and its affiliated mass organizations, such as the Committees for the Defense of the Revolution, the Cuban Confederation of Labor, the Union of Young Communists, and the children's Pioneers, reached down and controlled the citizenry at the neighborhood, workplace, school, university, and family levels. As Castro's charisma eroded after his 1970 harvest failure, and as the earlier voluntarism and enthusiasm of the citizenry began to slacken, the totalitarian state apparatus filled the breach through various forms of coercion, whereby the populace was continually mobilized in support of the regime.

The fourth major pillar of regime support was the Soviet Union. Soviet economic and military assistance enabled the Castro regime to survive in the face of U.S. hostility and hemispheric isolation during the 1960s and into the 1970s. Moscow's largesse increased after the Revolutionary Armed Forces mounted successful military expeditions that advanced Soviet interests in southern Africa (Angola) and the Horn (Ethiopia and the Ogaden) in the mid- to late-1970s. From that point onward, Cuba enjoyed a preferential relationship with the Soviet Union as a super–client-state, obtaining loans, credits, and subsidized prices for its sugar exports and oil imports, as well as technical and military assistance. As a consequence, Cuba became highly dependent on the U.S.S.R. to such an extent that Soviet economic ties to the island amounted to $4.3 billion annually during the 1986–1990 period—or more than 21 percent of Cuba's gross national product (GNP) (Pérez-López, 2001, pp. 44–45).

Surviving the Crisis of the 1990s

The disappearance of the Soviet Union in 1991 removed the Castro regime's external pillar of support and, in the process, created an ideological and economic crisis that reverberated through both the political elite and populace alike. The loss of Cuba's patron also weakened the other remaining pillars of regime support.

Perhaps in a manner unequalled since the 1970 harvest failure, Fidel Castro's moral authority and political sagacity were tarnished by the Soviet Union's collapse. Having literally hitched Cuba's fate to the Soviet star for more than three decades, the *comandante* was now perceived to be on the wrong side of history. His regime was left without its ideological lodestar and economic lifeline, with Cuba appearing alone and adrift in a post-communist world. Making matters worse was the fact that Cuba's great *caudillo,* along with his old-guard followers, stubbornly opposed the kind of deep, liberalizing economic reforms that had transformed China in the 1980s under the leadership of Deng Xiao Ping.

For Castro to have fully reversed economic course, however, would have been a tacit admission that he had been wrong in imposing a command-economy on Cuba, thus compromising his self-ascribed role in history. Hence, he limited the liberalizing reforms that he was compelled to take in the mid-1990s to a few half-measures—opening Cuba to foreign investments and tourism, allowing self-employment, dollarizing the economy,[2] replacing state farms with cooperatives, and permitting the return of farmers' markets. But then, once the economy began to right itself beginning in 1996, he stopped or reversed the reform process and removed or otherwise marginalized reformist leaders. With that reversal, it became clear that "Change with Fidel," a formula that it seems most Cubans would have preferred, had become an illusion.[3]

Although the *caudillo* continued to wield undisputed power and could count on support from segments of the populace, he no longer was immune from criticism. Cubans began to see him more and more as "*el viejo*" or "*el loco*"—a crazed leader out of touch with their everyday reality. No longer was he "Fidel," the young, inspirational leader of the past, but "Castro," the aging *caudillo* who cared only about his power and legacy.[4]

Meanwhile, the collapse of communism worldwide undermined another pillar of support: the Revolution. The Revolution had lost its ideological underpinnings and links to what had once been a universal, historic movement—a development that was particularly unsettling to the regime's elite. For ordinary Cubans, too, the Revolution no longer held out promise of a better economic future as the island's

---

[2] Enacted in mid-1993, this measure permitted Cubans to hold hard currency legally. It aimed at stemming the burgeoning black market and at capturing dollar remittances from Cuban exiles to their families and friends.

[3] "Change with Fidel" was proposed by Rafael Hernández, a Cuban economist, in his address, "Cuba Today: Economic and Political Challenges," Latin American Center, UCLA, January 11, 1993.

[4] This juxtaposition of "Fidel" the young leader and "Castro" the old *caudillo* was made by Marifeli Pérez-Stable in an informal conversation with one of the authors (Gonzalez) and three Cuban communist intellectuals at a symposium at Carleton University in Ottawa, Canada, in September 1993. None of the Cubans took issue with her characterization of the Cuban leader's transformation. George Plinio Montalván recounts that during his 1997 visit to Cuba, several people referred to the recent creation of agricultural cooperatives (*Unidades Basicas de Produción Cooperativa* [UBPCs]) as "*ultima bobería del Presidente Castro*" (the latest stupidity by President Castro). September 5, 2003, note to authors.

gross domestic product (GDP) plummeted by nearly 32 percent by 1993 compared with that of 1989. Cubans now had to endure unrelenting austerity under the "Special Period in a Time of Peace" that was launched in 1990 and that remains in effect today. Monthly food rations were cut back to a ten-day supply, forcing Cubans to grow their own vegetables and to scour the black market for food and other basic necessities that the government no longer could supply. Housing and transportation deteriorated sharply, as did public health—the crown jewel of Cuba's extensive social safety net. Unemployment as well as underemployment rose. As a result, the social compact between state and society became badly frayed as the economy shrank at an annual rate of –1.2 percent in the 1990–2000 period. Even if the economy were to maintain the 3.3-percent annual average growth rate of 1994–2002, Cubans will not regain their 1989 standard of living until 2009, according to a leading economic specialist on Cuba (Mesa-Lago, 2003b, p. 2). But the recovery may take longer: The Center for the Study of the Cuban Economy (CSCE), which is affiliated with the Cuban government, announced that 2003 would be "a difficult year" because the economy was expected to grow at a rate of only 1.5 percent (Cuba Transition Project, 2003b).

In the meantime, bereft of ideology and with the economy contracting after 1989, the totalitarian state apparatus—the regime's last supportive pillar—no longer could be sustained in its original form. As shortages and living conditions worsened, the state was unable to rely on police officers or Party or Committee for the Defense of the Revolution (CDR) militants to enforce public conformity because they were now increasingly susceptible to accepting bribes offered by equally desperate citizens. Because the state was no longer able to employ the labor force fully or supply consumers with basic necessities, Cubans turned to the proliferating black market and other illicit activities—from prostitution to the pilfering of government stores and warehouses—to survive on a day-to-day basis.

As the crisis of the 1990s unfolded, Cuba evolved into a post-totalitarian state—a mutant form of totalitarianism in which the state was less ideologically driven, less able to satisfy the basic needs of its citizens, and less able to fully penetrate, control, and mobilize society.

With ideology in disarray and the economy imploding, the boundaries of the post-totalitarian state receded, thereby opening up social and economic space to an emerging, incipient civil society.

For the first time, the Roman Catholic Church and Caritas, its humanitarian organization, engaged in charitable activities in competition with the state. The Catholic and protestant churches and Afro-Cuban sects gained believers as Cubans turned from Marxism to religion. The self-employed (*cuentapropistas*) were legalized, because the state no longer could provide full employment or satisfy consumer needs. Independent libraries and self-help associations, along with independent trade union leaders, economists, and journalists, sprang up throughout the island.

But while the Castro regime ceded some social and economic space under post-totalitarianism, it refused to cede *political* space. On the contrary, the regime employed the repressive apparatus of the old totalitarian order to ensure its continued monopoly of political power through a combination of low-intensity repression and, when necessary, open repression. Traditional mechanisms of control—State Security and the police within the Ministry of Interior, and the CDRs—were thus augmented by the newly formed Rapid Response Brigades of club-wielding workers to suppress dissidents, human-rights activists, and other emerging civil-society actors.

With the arrival of the new century, if not before, the Castro regime had surprised its critics and enemies by riding out the crisis that had been prompted by the collapse of its former patron. Except for major public demonstrations and riots in 1993 and 1994, it succeeded in stemming the tide of popular unrest. It was able to do so, in part, as a result of the government's limited economic reforms of the early to mid-1990s, which helped alleviate some of the most serious economic strains on the population. But, in addition, the regime survived precisely because it still retained a strong state apparatus, although one weaker than in the early years. The state was still supported by those sectors of the population whose lives had improved during the first decades of the Revolution, by those who remained personally committed to "Fidel," and by those whose careers and very lives were tied to the regime's surviving. And when needed, the state's security apparatus enabled the regime to suppress both organized political opposition and spontaneous street demonstrations while managing political dissent through harassment and other forms of low-intensity repression.

Clearing the Way for Regime Succession

Even as the regime demonstrated its staying power, the post-totalitarian state has opened up more space for society. The result is that citizens gradually became less compliant, even bolder in their political behavior. Capitalizing on their links to foreign nongovernment organizations (NGOs) and the Internet, for example, independent journalists emerged and began reporting on events inside Cuba that the government preferred to ignore or cover up. Independent librarians, many connected to protestant and evangelical denominations, set up small home libraries throughout the island, often incurring the wrath of local authorities. Then, in May 2002, under the leadership of the dissident Osvaldo Payá, the Varela Project collected more than 11,000 signatures, petitioning the National Assembly to enact political and economic reforms—something that would have been unimaginable under the former totalitarian order.

The regime responded harshly to these challenges to its authority. On March 18, 2003, State Security rounded up 75 dissidents, human-rights activists, and civil-society leaders, including independent librarians and no less than 26 independent journalists, all of whom were sentenced a month later to prison terms ranging from six to 28 years.[5] In a blistering speech on April 24, Castro blamed James

---

[5] Among the most prominent were Héctor Palacios, one of the top organizers of the Varela Project (27 years in prison); Oscar Elias Biscet, an Afro-Cuban follower of Martin Luther King, Jr., who had been released from prison in 2002 (25 years); Marta Beatriz Roque, an independent economist who also had been released from prison in 2002 (20 years); Oscar Espinosa Chepe, an independent economist (20 years); and Raúl Rivero, an independent journalist and accomplished poet (20 years). Osvaldo Payá was not arrested but remained under police surveillance; his political party was dismantled. The crackdown was the largest since the *Concilio Cubano* movement was crushed in February 1996.

Cason, the chief of the U.S. Interests Section in Havana, for inciting subversion through the mission's support for and material assistance to the dissidents, and warned that "we are going to implement our [anti-subversion] laws." In the meantime, on April 11, after a spate of hijackings, the government summarily executed three disaffected Afro-Cubans for having seized a ferryboat in a failed attempt to cross the Florida Straits. With world public opinion condemning the U.S. war in Iraq, the regime had reverted to a policy of open, heavy-handed repression reminiscent of that in the 1960s and that has shown no signs of abating.[6] In one fell swoop, it had succeeded in decimating the leadership of the political opposition and the nascent civil society while putting ordinary Cubans on notice that they had to toe the line or else.

The crackdown and executions sparked strong criticisms in Europe, which later caused Havana to withdraw its application for a trade and aid pact with the European Union, saying that European officials had imposed "unacceptable conditions" (David Gonzalez, 2003). Cuba was also condemned sharply by Latin American and especially European intellectuals and by human-rights NGOs—although not by the U.N. Commission on Human Rights.[7]

In the United States, the budding movement within Congress to lift the embargo and travel ban was stopped momentarily as even those sympathetic to the Cuban government, such as Congressman

---

[6] Families of those arrested and imprisoned have had their refrigerators and essential appliances confiscated, and their loved ones have been moved to prisons located in other parts of the island. Access to the Internet has also been tightened for ordinary citizens. Independent librarians and other civil-society leaders and human-rights activists who escaped the initial dragnet face heightened harassment and close monitoring by State Security agents. For a summary and update, see Cuba Transition Project (2003c).

[7] Headed by Libya, the 53-member Commission on April 29, 2003, reelected Cuba to a three-year term as part of the six-country slate selected by Latin America. Earlier, the Commission mildly rebuked Cuba by asking it to accept a U.N. human rights observer—a request that Havana later rejected. The Commission defeated a stronger amendment that referred to Havana's recent crackdown and that called for the release of the more than 75 imprisoned dissidents.

Charles Rangel, expressed public outrage.[8] For its part, the Bush administration expelled 14 Cuban diplomats from their Washington and U.N. missions, and severely curtailed cultural, artistic, and other U.S. exchanges to the island as of June 1, 2003.

On June 6, the European Union (EU) froze further consideration of the trade and aid pact with Cuba, limited high-level government visits to the island, and invited Cuban dissidents to Europe. On June 24, the Paris-based Reporters Without Borders issued a stinging indictment of the regime, charging that with its earlier imprisonment of four independent journalists, Cuba had now become "the world's biggest prison for members of the press" (Reporters Without Borders, 2003a, p. 1; 2003b).[9] In the meantime, in mid-June, Castro and his brother Raúl led mass marches past the Spanish and Italian Embassies to protest the EU's stance, and the Cuban leader later insulted the Spanish and Italian prime ministers by name.[10] And on July 26, the fiftieth anniversary of the start of the Cuban Revolution, Castro again lashed out at the EU for its "arrogance" and at Spanish Prime Minister José María Aznar for his "markedly fascist lineage and ideology."[11]

As has occurred on numerous occasions since 1959, the March 18 crackdown and subsequent events demonstrate that, for Castro, economics are to be subordinated to the overriding priorities of power and politics. With the island's economic situation again deteriorating, he was willing to antagonize the EU, which is Cuba's largest international investor and trading partner, when with one pre-

---

[8] However, on September 9, 2003, the U.S. House of Representatives voted once again to lift the travel ban by a 227-188 vote (compared with the 262-167 tally in 2002). If the Senate follows suit, the bill may be killed in the conference committee or, if not, it is likely to be vetoed by President Bush.

[9] The media watchdog group launched a summer campaign to dissuade European tourists from vacationing in Cuba.

[10] In a three-hour TV address on June 14, Castro accused the two prime ministers of instigating the EU sanctions against Cuba, and called the EU statement a "heap of trash." He referred to Spanish Prime Minister José María Aznar as a "little fuhrer with a little mustache" and called Italy's premier "Benito Burlesconi."

[11] Speech given by Fidel Castro on July 26, 2003, "Cuba Does Not Need the European Union to Survive and Develop."

emptive strike he decapitated the ranks of the political opposition (Bond, 2003, p. 123):

> The recent crackdown has left Cuba's most courageous civil-society activists in jail for decades (three others arrested in the same roundup are still awaiting trial). . . . Those behind bars come from all races and walks of life: Catholics and Freemasons, intellectuals and peasants. Some are only in their twenties; others are in their sixties. Less than half of the prisoners lived in Havana—proof that their cause represents not an elite occupation but a broader movement, albeit one now decapitated.

Adhering to his usual modus operandi, he sought to mobilize public support and justify his crackdown on dissidents by raising the specter of a U.S. invasion of Cuba—this time by broadcasting European and Arab television coverage of the Iraqi War and by ordering air-raid drills at primary schools. But the aging leader may also have had a longer-term objective in mind in launching the March 18, 2003, dragnet: to ensure that his anointed, successor communist regime can take power without having to confront an internal political opposition. That way, both his place in history and his Revolution would survive his passing.

The Outlook for a Successor Communist Regime

A successor communist regime that takes power after Castro departs the scene will initially possess a number of political advantages. It will inherit the apparatus of the post-totalitarian state, whereas the political opposition, now largely shattered, is likely to remain weak along with what little there is of civil society. It will control the state's coercive instruments of power—the Revolutionary Armed Forces (FAR), the Ministry of Interior (MININT), the 780,000-member Communist Party of Cuba, and the millions who belong to the PCC-controlled mass organizations, such as the CDRs.

As his elder brother's designated successor, Raúl Castro has had his anointment further strategically buttressed by his control over both the FAR and MININT. However, even if he outlives his brother,[12] Raúl lacks Fidel's personal magnetism and moral authority, has little visible public support of his own, and is an unlikely candidate as another *caudillo*. He will need to compensate for his weaknesses by presiding over a coalition of *fidelista* and *raulista* loyalists of both hard-line and centrist orientation, from which the reformists, at least initially, are likely to be excluded.[13] But whatever its composition, the new regime is likely to find itself crippled from the outset by the loss of two out of the three remaining pillars of support—Fidel and the Revolution—because only the apparatus of the post-totalitarian state will remain in place.

The successor regime will be weakened in the first instance by the absence of the *comandante,* who in 2003 is still able to infuse his regime with legitimacy, direction, and cohesiveness. With his passing, the popular legitimacy that was invested in his person will be gone. The regime could well become rudderless as factions emerge and struggle for power and authority in the absence of his unifying presence. If the regime falters, then the military is likely to step in and rule directly.[14]

Second, the Revolution no longer is the great legitimizing force that it once was. Although reliable attitudinal survey data are unavailable, the Revolution has surely become a disillusioning experience for millions of Cubans. Especially under the Special Period that began in

---

[12] Raúl turned 72 years of age in June 2003; Fidel became 77 the following August. However, Raúl is not in the best of health. Were he to leave the scene before Fidel, his passing would greatly upset succession dynamics and calculations while also removing a constraining, pragmatic influence on Fidel.

[13] One clue as to the coalition's future composition is in the new 31-member Council of State, which was approved by Cuba's National Assembly on March 6, 2003. Handpicked by Fidel, at least one-third of the new Council was made up of old *fidelista* and *raulista* followers who date back to the anti-Batista struggle. The reappointment of Economics and Planning Minister José Luis Rodríguez, who is not a reformer, is one more indication that the regime intends to continue holding out against liberalizing reforms even as the island's economic situation is worsening.

[14] On elite divisions and how different succession scenarios may play out, see Edward Gonzalez (2002a).

1990, the government has been unable to fulfill its part of the social compact (a critical element of the Revolution):

- Food shortages and material scarcities abound.
- Health care and other public services have sharply deteriorated—although Cuba still has registered favorable statistics in infant mortality and adult human immunodeficiency virus (HIV) rates.[15] Nevertheless, basic medicines became unavailable, and hospitals and clinics became physically deteriorated, except for facilities catering to foreigners, who received first-class treatment under Cuba's "medical tourism" program to capture hard currency.
- Education has become superfluous. Teachers, doctors, and other professionals have abandoned their peso-denominated, low-paying careers in the state sector to earn dollars as taxi-drivers, small entrepreneurs, hustlers, and prostitutes.
- Social equity has been replaced by vast income inequalities. Pensioners and workers in the public sector are paid in devalued pesos; they earn far less than those who have access to exile remittances or work in the private sector, where they earn dollars.[16]

The Revolution has also failed to fulfill its nationalist promise. Prior to 1989, Cuba had become so dependent economically upon the Soviet Union that its situation turned nearly catastrophic

---

[15] At 7 deaths per 1,000 births in 1999, Cuba's infant mortality rate is comparable to that of the developed world. Cuba also has by far the lowest HIV prevalence rate among adults in the Caribbean. Cuba's rate was 0.1 percent of the 15-to-49-year-old population in 2000. The next-lowest rate was in Jamaica (1.2 percent) and Barbados (1.2 percent), whereas the Dominican Republic had 2.5-percent and Haiti had 6.1-percent rates. *The New York Times*, May 18, 2003, p. 10.

[16] According to data compiled by Mesa-Lago (2003a, p. 5) for monthly income in Havana for March–April 2002, a pensioner earned the equivalent of as little as $4; an elementary and secondary school teacher, $8–$15; a university professor, $12–$22; an officer in the armed forces, $13–$23; and a cabinet minister, $17–$23. In contrast, working in the private sector, a farmer earned $77–$1,923; a prostitute, $240–$1,400; a landlord renting a room, apartment, or house, $250–$4,000; and an owner of a *paladar* (home restaurant), $12,500–$50,000 (although the upper-range figure was rare).

once the Soviet lifeline was severed. Then, in the 1990s, Cuba had to turn to foreign investors and tourism to stanch the economy's hemorrhaging. Foreign investments at least provided employment, although foreign or joint enterprises do not pay the workers directly: They pay a state agency a monthly amount per worker in hard currency, and then the state agency pays the worker in pesos, which amounts to about a 95 percent confiscation of the wage. But, perhaps more galling to nationalist-minded Cubans is that they have become second-class citizens in their own country: Unless they are accompanied by a foreigner, they are denied access to tourist resorts, beaches, nightclubs, restaurants, and dollar shops—even when they possess hard currency. Under medical apartheid, Cubans have also been denied first-rate health care, which is reserved for hard-currency-paying foreigners, who are lured to the island under the government's policy of "medical tourism." Worse yet, to earn hard currency, women and girls as young as 12 or 13 have turned to having sex with European, Latin, and North American men flocking to the island.

After more than four decades of Revolution, therefore, Cuba was returning to the maligned pre-Revolutionary Cuba. Even Castro's efforts to burnish what remains of the Revolution's luster could not paper over the Revolution's recent failures, because those failures were being experienced directly by individuals and their families. Not surprisingly, there appears to be widespread public exhaustion and disillusionment with the Revolution. Especially among the younger generation, as Damiàn Fernàndez (2004, Appendix B) points out, there is a yearning for change that leads to a more normal life. Hence, with Castro's passing, if not before, it is likely that the Revolution will have ceased to be a legitimizing force that could serve as a pillar of support for a successor regime.

What Castro's heirs will have at their disposal is the post-totalitarian state apparatus. But this apparatus may well serve as a two-edged sword: Even as it enhances the regime's security, it deprives the regime of needed popular legitimacy. In fact, the Castro regime's March 18 crackdown on dissidents, along with the execution of the three Afro-Cuban hijackers, reportedly has further alienated ordinary citizens from the regime. Concern is even being voiced among some members of the elite, who question the wisdom of the new repressive line that Castro and other hard-liners have adopted.[17] Consequently, reliance on the post-totalitarian state's control apparatus is certain to delegitimize the successor regime, because that reliance will signify that political repression constitutes the only pillar of support available to the new regime.

To legitimize itself, therefore, a communist successor regime will need to promote the island's economic recovery and reconstruction. But here, Castro's twin legacies of caudilloism and totalitarianism are likely to weaken the new regime politically, impeding its ability to consider needed reforms and embark upon a new economic course.

The Burden of Caudilloism on a Successor Communist Regime

The most immediate problem that a successor communist regime will face is: Who can fill the *comandante*'s shoes now that he is gone? Cuba's *caudillo* has jealously guarded his power by getting rid of potential rivals—executing Division General Arnaldo Ochoa in 1989, then purging Foreign Minister Roberto Robaina in 1999. Of the remaining contenders, neither Raúl nor others, such as economics czar Carlos Lage, National Assembly President Ricardo Alarcón, or Foreign Minister Felipe Pérez Roque, possess Fidel's commanding presence or enjoy mass support of their own. Each will find it difficult to reign in what is likely to be intensified infighting among competing elites after Fidel Castro departs. And without strong leadership and

---

[17] Elizardo Sánchez Santa Cruz, head of the Cuban Commission on Human Rights and National Reconciliation, claims that the crackdown on dissident and opposition leaders has won those leaders support on the streets. In "Preocupa a Comunistas Jóvenes la represión en Cuba" (2003), *Contacto Magazine* reports an interview with two Cuban officials from the Ministry of Foreign Affairs who are in their early 40s, who said their generation was "preoccupied and disoriented" by the crackdown and executions, which recalled the worst excesses of the Revolution's radical period in the 1960s. They considered the action by Castro and other hard-liners a major strategic mistake that left Cuba isolated and in danger of an attack from the United States. One even wondered whether U.S. troops would be welcomed as liberators in Cuba as they were in Iraq.

elite cohesion, the chances are slim that the new regime can embark upon a new economic course.

The leadership void could be filled institutionally, but Castro's personalistic style of governance has been such that there has always existed a tension between caudilloism and institutionalization. Even with the so-called institutionalization of the Revolution, which commenced in the 1970s, the Cuban leader used the reinvigorated Party apparatus and the new 1976 Constitution to formalize his already-formidable powers as Commander in Chief, First Secretary of the Party, and head of both state and government. The question thus arises: Can the existing institutional arrangements transcend his passing and assume an institutional coherence and legitimacy of their own?

In this respect, institutional governance under Castro has been essentially pro forma over the past 30 years. The National Assembly of People's Power normally meets but twice a year for two-day sessions, during which it obediently ratifies the laws and decrees issued in the interim by the Council of State. The Party Congresses are largely scripted events, and in recent years they have not been convened as regularly prescribed.[18] Hand-picked by the Castro brothers, the Party's Political Bureau and Central Committee serve as instruments for wielding the uncontested political power at the top, while Party secretaries and committees at the provincial levels ensure that their orders are carried out by lower Party and state echelons.

With its cadres of 780,000, the PCC is designated constitutionally as Cuba's sovereign, guiding institution. For that reason, the PCC is a select organization rather than a mass party open to ordinary citizens; its candidates are carefully screened for their loyalty, ideological commitment, and political dedication. But the Party experienced an extraordinary surge in membership from 1992 to 1996, when 232,457 new members were enrolled, which suggests that recruiting standards were lowered in order to boost the Party's rolls in a

---

[18] Although they are to be held every five years, both the Fourth and Fifth Party Congresses were delayed by a year as a result of the crisis of the 1990s, whereas the Sixth Party Congress had also been postponed from December 2002 to an unannounced time in 2003 or 2004.

time of acute crisis. If so, many may have joined for opportunistic reasons: to get ahead precisely when the economy was failing because Party membership is required for managerial positions in the joint- and state-owned enterprises doing business in the tourist and other hard-currency sectors of the economy. The Party, then, may be becoming a vehicle for personal advancement and enrichment, and less of a professionalized instrument for governance. Whether the Party can retain legitimacy in the eyes of the populace under such circumstances, particularly after Castro is gone, appears problematic.

Castro's passing, therefore, is likely to produce a leadership void in terms not only of personalities but also of institutions, which could well have a degenerative, delegitimizing effect on the successor regime. With 75 percent of the Political Bureau having been appointed since 1989, the Party's leaders ". . . expect to govern Cuba after Castro's passing, and they believe they can govern it effectively according to their preferences. . . . [T]hey believe that no new significant economic reforms are necessary because the recovery is on course" (Domínguez, 2002). But if their authority is questioned in the *comandante*'s absence and/or their failure to produce economic results, there could be challengers who will mobilize their own institutional power base—for example, in the National Assembly or the Revolutionary Armed Forces. Were such a power struggle to break out, the regime would find its capacity to lead greatly debilitated.

Even if individual and institutional lines of succession are adhered to, the new regime will still be dogged by Castro's caudillioistic legacy, because his populist policies attracted a wide public following. The number and intensity of his followers have diminished with time, especially since the Special Period was implemented; however, committed *fidelistas* are still to be found inside and outside the current government, and they will expect his successors to be true to his populist legacy. Like the *peronista* movement in post-Peron Argentina, therefore, they are likely to become an important—although, for the most part, aging—political force in a post-Castro Cuba, and their demands cannot safely be ignored by the new regime. This force, in turn, is certain to present Castro's successors with a major dilemma: If they emulate the kind of populist appeals that served the great *caudillo* well, which might help them politically, they will undermine their efforts to revive the economy.

A case in point is Castro's ultra-nationalist, defiant postures, which enabled him to manipulate public opinion, blame the economy's troubles on the U.S. embargo, and repeatedly re-equilibrate the political system so that Cubans remained in a state of permanent tension and mobilization. Raúl and other leaders in the successor regime would surely be inclined to adopt a similar nationalist stance for the same political reasons. Such a stance would also ensure support from the regime's old guard, the younger Communist Party militants, members of the army and internal security forces, and sectors of the population for whom Castro's nationalist appeals symbolized the very essence of the Revolution.

But while ultra-nationalism would make for good domestic politics, it could be ruinous for the economy and, in the end, self-destructive to the successor regime itself. Without the traditional pillars of support to sustain it, the regime will be in desperate need of economic support from the international community at all levels—governmental, private sector, and multinational institutions. Even if the United States does not restore bilateral diplomatic and economic relations, it will still be the key player in influencing the extent to which other international actors provide economic assistance, credits, and investments to a post-Castro Cuba. Continued tension between Washington and Havana, for example, would add to international uncertainties, including among foreign banks and investors, as to whether the successor regime could long survive continued U.S. hostility and isolation. Hence, renewed anti-imperialist, anti-American rhetoric, along with anti-democratic practices on the part of the successor regime, will surely leave a post-Castro Cuba not only in conflict with the United States but also more economically vulnerable than ever.

Another populist appeal that is certain to present problems for a post-Castro communist regime is the *fidelista* pursuit of a moral economy based on equality, a classless society, and non-materialism. Under Castro's moral economy, private enrichment became a sin, social equity became enshrined, and vast income disparities were eliminated. For example, even today, a cabinet minister receives a monthly income of only 600 pesos. Of course, until the dollarization of the economy in 1993, it was political power—which still remains tightly rationed—and not lucre that enabled the regime's "new class" to enjoy a standard of living well beyond the reach of ordinary citizens, who remained virtually powerless. In compensation, the general populace received equitably distributed "social goods"—employment, health care, education, subsidized housing, food rations—and became socialized in the norms and expectations of socioeconomic equality.

The principle of a moral economy was upended with the onset of the crisis of the 1990s, which forced the government to enact modest liberalizing reforms that produced growing social stratification and inequality. Income disparities have increased dramatically between those Cubans who possessed dollars because they were in the new economy and those who remained in the traditional economy and who had to survive on peso-denominated wages and salaries worth 20–25 pesos to the dollar (Mesa-Lago, 2003a). The principal beneficiaries of the new economy are workers in the tourist industry and joint enterprises, the self-employed, and those who ply the black market, rent out rooms, serve as prostitutes, and receive exile remittances. Left in the traditional, peso-denominated economy are state employees, Party workers, military and security personnel, and pensioners. Included in the latter category, too, are the majority of Afro-Cubans who, for one reason or another, including unofficial discrimination, have largely been left out of the new economy even though they are estimated to make up upward of 50 percent of the population.

As disgruntlement over the increasing inequalities intensified among the regime's traditional constituencies, and despite some signs of economic recovery, Castro halted the reforms in 1996. The government actively discouraged self-employment through harassment, high taxes, and a new law against "improper enrichment." The result was that the number of self-employed owning micro-enterprises fell 63 percent between 1997 and 2001, from 209,000 to an estimated 150,000. The absence of reformers from the recent appointments to

Council of Ministers and the Party's Political Bureau suggests that the Castro regime will continue to hew to its present course.

A successor communist regime will thus be faced with a Hobson's Choice after the great *caudillo* is gone. If the regime adheres to the *fidelista* precepts and normative values of a moral economy, it probably will retain the backing of traditional Castro loyalists, but doing so could well come at the expense of revitalizing the economy. However, if it reverses course and lays off excess workers in state enterprises, and actively promotes the growth of small, private entrepreneurs and farmers, steps required for the island's economic recovery, militants in the Party, FAR, MININT, and general populace could be alienated.[19] Choosing the latter course would thus require a strong state—one that is not likely to be in place after Castro is gone.

The Burden of Totalitarianism on Society

Even if a post-Castro successor regime were to muster the will to enact market-friendly policies for both Cubans and foreigners alike, it would still be saddled with Cuba's totalitarian legacy as a lawless state in spite of the countless laws the government has enacted since 1959. What has been missing all along is the rule of law in which laws and regulations

- are binding and equally enforced with respect to the conduct of both rulers and the general populace
- are not arbitrarily and retroactively applied
- provide for government transparency and accountability.

In Cuba, laws have been ignored, changed, or repealed to suit the interests of Castro and his regime, such as what occurred with the

---

[19] These steps refer to the pursuit of a genuine market economy. In contrast, the FAR in particular would likely favor continuing with Cuba's present patrimonial state or with adopting the Chinese model, because in both the state entrusts the military with control over some key industries.

1989 execution of Division General Arnaldo Ochoa and Colonel Tony De la Guardia under circumstances reminiscent of the Stalinist purge trials of the 1930s.[20] Later, starting in the mid-1990s, the regime deliberately subverted the self-employment decree. Most recently, in April 2003, it preemptively and unlawfully executed three young blacks who had attempted to hijack a ferryboat.[21]

Cuba is thus without the kind of stable, predictable, lawful environment necessary for sustained investment and risk-taking on the part of businessmen, and for society itself to become law abiding. In fact, the contrary has occurred: As in the former Soviet Union and Eastern bloc countries, Cubans have been obliged to violate the law by resorting to black-market activities, pilfering state stores and warehouses, and engaging in still other illegal activities in order to survive from day to day during the Special Period. Hence, not only the state but society as well will need to internalize the rule of law over time if a post-Castro Cuba is to cease being a lawless state (for further elaboration, see Patillo Sánchez, 2003).

The legacy of totalitarianism/post-totalitarianism is likely to leave still another, dysfunctional imprint on society that may take generations to erase. This imprint is reflected in the very structure of society, as well as in individual attitudes and values conditioned by more than 40 years of rule by the Castro regime.

At the structural level, Cuba lacks a civil society comparable to what existed in Eastern Europe and the Soviet Union prior to the

---

[20] The execution of Ochoa and De la Guardia, together with their two assistants, shocked the Cuban elite and society alike. The show trial found Ochoa and De la Guardia guilty of money-laundering and drug-trafficking, leading many outside experts to believe the charges had been trumped up to cover up the Cuban government's own complicity in drug-trafficking. However, De la Guardia's son-in-law, Jorge Massetti, argues that they were executed because they admired Gorbachev's policies of *glasnost* and *perestroika,* which they wanted to see adopted in Cuba. See Jorge Massetti's memoir, *In the Pirate's Den—My Life as a Secret Agent for Castro,* San Francisco, Calif.: Encounter Books, 2003.

[21] According to Cuban law, the death penalty is to be applied only in the most grievous cases, and not as a measure of prevention. In the ferryboat incident, no one was injured, the hijackers surrendered peaceably, and they showed repentance. In a 1994 attempted hijacking, in which a policeman was killed, the death penalty was not applied to the perpetrator (Colas, 2003).

collapse of communism, largely because of the strength and policies of Castro's totalitarian/post-totalitarian state.[22] With a few exceptions such as the Catholic Church, no intermediary, autonomous institution exists to serve as a buffer between the individual, the family, and the community on the one hand, and the all-powerful state and Party on the other. The Castro government has prevented such a civil society from forming, with the result that only a "proto–civil society" has emerged, largely at the informal level, consisting of ". . . small and not so small groups and institutions [including some within the state] articulating different interests and identities outside the control of the Party-state" (Fernández, 2001, p. 60). The March 18, 2003, crackdown has now decimated much of the leadership of this emerging proto–civil society, leaving the regime once again fully in control.

Such a state of affairs could facilitate a successor regime taking power without major opposition, thus making the emergence of a future democratic polity even more remote. In turn, this outcome would perpetuate the self-steering character of the present Cuban state into the future, because society would be left without the autonomous organizations and institutions by which to influence the successor regime's public policies, including in the areas of economic strategy and national reconciliation.

Cuba's totalitarian/post-totalitarian order has also exacerbated cleavages within society, and in political attitudes, norms, and practices. A civic, democratic political culture never came to fruition during the history of the Republic (1902–1959); however, Castro's new order produced the "institutionalization of intolerance" after 1959 (Fernandez, 2003a). Cubans became divided between the

---

[22] A major determinant of civil society is whether the state accepts it or is too weak to prevent its rise. In the Eastern bloc, the state in most cases had ceased to be totalitarian and was too weak and illegitimate to crush the established Catholic Church (Poland, Hungary) and protestant church (East Germany) or new civil-society actors, such as Solidarity (Poland) and student and intellectual groups (Czechoslovakia, East Germany). Beginning with the Brezhnev era, the Soviet Union's sclerotic post-totalitarian state was unable to squelch the rise of the dissident movement and underground press. With Gorbachev's emergence as a reformer after 1985, civil-society actors proliferated under a more benign state. For a discussion of the commonalties and differences between Cuba and other communist states, see Gonzalez and Szayna (1998).

committed *fidelista* majority (at that time) and those less committed or opposed to the government, with the latter finding themselves placed "outside the Revolution"—in other words, outside the national community in the eyes of both the regime and much of the population. Either out of conviction or to protect themselves, Cubans became the state's accomplices in policing their neighbors, fellow workers, families, and even themselves to assure widespread societal conformity and compliance with the government.

The crisis of the 1990s, and the resulting rise in public protests and political dissent, further set Cubans against Cubans as the regime used its Rapid Response Brigades, its ubiquitous Committees for the Defense of the Revolution, and its legions of informers against its critics and opponents. With the March 18 crackdown, tension between state and society, and between ordinary Cubans, appears to be intensifying as evidenced by both the government's heightened repression and the surge in the number of Cubans trying to flee the island.[23]

A communist successor regime, therefore, is certain to be faced with a deeply polarized society. The major fault line will run between committed *fidelistas*, who at most may constitute a large minority bloc, and the rest of the population, whose attitudes are likely to range from indifference to seething hatred toward Castro's successors. As occurred in the East European communist transitions, this polarization is certain to tear at Cuba's social fabric all the way down to the grass-roots level. Indeed, many Cubans are as likely to want to settle scores with the neighbor or co-worker who snitched on them as they are to want justice meted out to MININT and Party officials who abused their power.

However, Castro's communist successors are unlikely to provide them with satisfaction on either score. They are also unlikely to prove capable of promoting national reconciliation because of their own totalitarian inclinations and previous culpability in repressing the

---

[23] Between October 1, 2002, and July 24, 2003, the number of Cubans intercepted at sea by the U.S. Coast Guard had jumped to 1,178 compared with 666 for the entire 12-month period from October 1, 2001, through September 30, 2002 (Dahlburg, 2003, p. A-15).

population. Without a democratic transition, therefore, prospects for national reconciliation are dim, with the result that a communist successor regime will likely have to preside over a divided Cuba.

And a post-Castro society may not simply be politically polarized. Many, if not the vast majority, of Cubans may wish to disengage from politics all together, precisely because of the degree to which Cuba's totalitarian/post-totalitarian order sowed pervasive societal mistrust (*desconfianza*) and politicized everyday life. For decades, Cubans have had to employ their *cara doble* (literally, two faces) to conceal their real thoughts and sentiments from each other as well as from the authorities. They have become increasingly aware, too, of the *doble moral* (double, or hypocritical, morality), in which their government's highly touted public morality—often expressed by Castro in terms of taking a "principled" position—diverged from its actual conduct. Already there are signs that Cubans are reacting to these forms of behavior by retreating from politics. As Damián J. Fernández (2004, Appendix B) notes, much of Cuba's youth have become "desocialized"—and thus disconnected—from officially sanctioned dogmas and norms as evidenced by their consciously taking up alternative or Western lifestyles or engaging in proscribed activities. Weary of politics, older Cubans also appear to yearn for a more normal life, albeit with the preservation of the social safety net.

A politically withdrawn, self-absorbed society poses problems for the perpetuation of a post-totalitarian order after Castro is gone. Granted, a disengaged society will present less political opposition to a communist successor regime, but it will also be a society that is more difficult to mobilize and whose energies will be more difficult to channel along prescribed lines, as the Castro regime itself has discovered in recent years. The changing character of Cuban society may thus already be leading to the obsolescence of the post-totalitarian order in the years ahead.

Hence, a communist successor regime is likely to find itself trapped in a cul-de-sac that, at best, promises stasis for a post-Castro Cuba and, at worst, poses growing political instability, heightened social anomie, and a prolonged economic impasse. The conditions under which Castro was able to rule as Latin America's (and the world's) longest-reigning *caudillo*, and which favored the extended control of the totalitarian state apparatus over the economy and society, no longer exist. A post-Castro communist regime will thus have to erect new mechanisms and policies if it is to survive for long, a task that will be further compounded by the structural problems that lie ahead for Cuba, as will be discussed below.

The Democratic and Military Alternative

A non-communist successor government, of course, would be less hobbled by the ideological strictures and political stances associated with the *fidelista* legacy. Such a government would have to maintain elements of the country's social safety net in order to attract popular support. But freed of *fidelista* ideology and political baggage from the past, it would be better positioned to begin replacing the state-controlled economy with a more market-oriented economy, one that encourages the rise of small, privately owned businesses and farms, rewards individual initiative, and accepts the accumulation of private wealth as a necessary additive for boosting economic growth. A non-communist government could also be free to launch Cuba on the path of a democratic transition. However, a democratic polity would also make the government susceptible to rejection by the electorate if it is unable to govern effectively, improve the economy, and raise the living standards of the majority of the people.

At present, a democratic successor government appears more remote than ever. Castro's followers control the instruments of state power, and other conditions essential to democratic governance are lacking in Cuba. With the March 18 crackdown, the prospects for a robust civil society—a key requisite for democratic government—have been dealt a grievous setback. Also, a politically withdrawn, self-absorbed society, particularly among Cuba's youth, would not provide the political participation and support needed to sustain a democratic government—a situation made worse if politics are left to the more committed *fidelistas*—communist militants whose calling is politics. Additionally, contending political elites and the general population have not been socialized in democratic norms and practices and the rule of law. Even if the democratic opposition could gain power, it is likely to be saddled with a *fidelista-raulista* military establishment that is not only anti-democratic in its value orientation but also has a strong stake in perpetuating the existing political and economic order after Castro is gone.

The Revolutionary Armed Forces, in fact, are certain to be the key institution in determining Cuba's future after Castro has departed the scene. As the successor to the Rebel Army that overthrew Batista, the FAR predates the establishment of Castro's new Communist Party in 1965 and thus possesses a revolutionary legitimacy the PCC does not enjoy. Under the direction of Raúl Castro, it became a professionalized military that successfully waged a counterinsurgency campaign on the island in the 1960s and engaged in large-scale combat missions in Africa in the 1970s and 1980s. All the while the FAR served as a loyal instrument of armed support for the Castro brothers, one that was pledged to defend the regime, the Revolution, and the Fatherland.

Hence, the Ochoa affair and the FAR's severe downsizing as a result of the economic contraction of the 1990s notwithstanding, the regime has continued to enjoy the military's support through the practices of the patrimonial state. Loyalty has been promoted largely by giving the FAR a major role in directing the more-lucrative sectors of the "new," or dollar, economy, such as tourism. For tourism, it operates wholly owned enterprises, such as the far-flung *Gaviota* complex, or participates in joint ventures with foreign capital. Additionally, six generals currently hold seats in the Party's 24-member Political Bureau, while senior officers have recently occupied high government and state positions.[24] As a result, much of the officer class has become a stakeholder in the present system by virtue of the

---

[24] In late 2001, FAR officers held 13 of the 37 seats in the Council of Ministers, according to Juan Carlos Espinosa (2001, p. 24). In the new 31-member Council of State approved by the National Assembly of People's Power in March 2003, senior generals held three positions, which may possibly signify a turn to civilian rather military leaders for the administration of non–defense-related government ministries.

FAR's strong institutional and personal interest in the management of both the state and the economy. Hence, it is likely to support a successor communist regime rather than a democratic one. Were the new communist leadership to falter after Castro is gone, the FAR most probably would step in and establish a military-led government similar to that of General Wojciech Jaruzelski in Poland in 1981–1989. Whether the FAR's cohesion and chain of command can be preserved if it directly assumes power remains to be seen.[25]

Strictly from a political perspective, therefore, Cuba's future looks grim, because the post-Castro state is likely to be weakened by the political legacies the *comandante* will have bequeathed to his successors. Neither a communist successor regime nor a more democratically inclined or military-led regime is likely to be able to escape the dysfunctional consequences of the past 44-plus years of caudilloism and totalitarianism/post-totalitarianism. The situation facing any one of these types of government looks even grimmer when the island's youth, race, demographic, and economic problems are factored in.

---

[25] Brian Latell (2003) points out that the FAR is likely to become increasingly exposed to four "cross-cutting fissures" in the post-Castro period that will weaken the cohesion of the military. These are (1) tension over the Ochoa affair, (2) generational stresses between the "younger Turk officers" and senior officers, (3) animosity between traditional troop commanders and their staff and the new "soldier entrepreneurs" who have benefited from for-profit activities, and (4) the erosion of professionalism due to corruption and a new class of wealthy officers.

CHAPTER THREE

Cuba's Disaffected Youth[1]

Background

Generations of Cuban youths have served as important catalysts in the country's political history. The Ten Years War (1868–1878), the War of Independence (1895–1898), and the 1933 revolution were ignited and led in the main by young nationalists. The attack on the Moncada Barracks on July 26, 1953, the opening shot in what would become the Cuban Revolution, was led by Fidel Castro when he was just under 27 years of age. Less than six years later, he had vaulted to power at the ripe age of 32. His brother Raúl was five years younger, and many other *barbudos* from the Rebel Army were younger still. Indeed, it is not an exaggeration to say that the Revolution constituted a generation break: Older, established politicians who had opposed Batista quickly found themselves shunted aside, with most going into exile during and after 1959. As the pace of revolutionary change quickened, younger leaders took over the new government, the increasingly state-owned economy, the print, radio, and TV media, the universities, and other nongovernmental organizations.

In the meantime, the Isle of Pines was renamed the Isle of Youth as young Cubans became the Revolution's shock troops during its first decades in power. Student volunteers spearheaded the government's campaign against illiteracy in the early 1960s. Afterwards, youngsters began to be sent to the *escuelas al campo* (schools in the

---

[1] This chapter is based on Fernández (2004, Appendix B).

countryside) to learn the value of agricultural work. Older youths served in the newly reconstituted Revolutionary Armed Forces, the Student Work Brigades, or the Youth Labor Army, which engaged in nation-building tasks. The most dedicated became members of the elite Union of Communist Youth. Meanwhile, students enrolled in technical schools and universities, from which they emerged as agronomists, teachers, technicians, and physicians, among other professions.

For Fidel Castro and other young rebels who came to power in 1959, Cuba's youth would be entrusted with ensuring the Revolution's everlasting triumph. Hence, through socialization in schools and other venues, the young would be transformed into Che Guevara's selfless "new communist man." Today, in fact, "good communist youth" can be found in the Party, whose ranks have swelled in recent years from the influx of young recruits, and in the retinue of personal assistants surrounding the Cuban leader.

Nevertheless, the mutually supportive relationship between the state and Cuba's *youth*—herein defined as constituting the 16-to-30-year-old age group—was not to last. The relationship began to deteriorate as early as the late 1970s. Tension between the state and its youth intensified after 1989 as the young were faced with heightened austerity, few opportunities for upward mobility, and unfulfilled personal aspirations—material, spiritual, and cultural. In response, more and more youths came to consciously reject official dogma and the regime's prescribed norms of behavior.

As Damián Fernández (2004) notes, the relationship between the state and youth has thus been marked in recent years by ". . . a history of unfulfilled aspirations and escalating tensions between the state and the young" consisting of "the state's frustration with the young, and the young's frustration with the state." Indeed, Cuba appears to be on the verge of once again experiencing a generation break as it did in the 1950s. Only, this time, the growing strain is between Fidel, Raúl, and other members of the original 1953 leadership generation, and the ranks of disenchanted, disillusioned, and rebellious youth. The problem with Cuba's disaffected youth is not confined to the current regime, however. It is certain to carry over to the post-

Castro period, during which it will present a major political challenge—along with other obstacles—to the viability of a successor government.

The Growing Alienation of *Los Jóvenes*

Many factors are contributing to the emerging generation break in today's Cuba. These can be divided into two analytic categories—internal root causes and exogenous accelerators—which have worked cumulatively over time to alienate Cuba's young.

One principal root cause lies in the high expectations held by the older leadership generation that it could mold the young—*los jóvenes*—into becoming the "new man." As early as March 1959, Fidel Castro declared that

> We need men of character and it is logical that this generation cannot be as good as future generations, because this generation was not educated in a revolutionary doctrine; it was not educated in good examples. *The formidable generation, the marvelous generation, will be the coming one; and that one will truly be more perfect than us.* (*Revolución*, March 13, 1959, p. 11. Emphasis added.)

The new man or woman was to personify selflessness, rejection of individualism and materialism, *conciencia* (revolutionary consciousness), egalitarianism, patriotism, internationalism, and loyalty to Fidel and the Revolution.

To achieve these highly idealized attributes, the young were systematically subjected at all ages to a vast array of socializing agents, starting with their state-run education. These agents consisted of preschools (*Círculos Infantiles,* or day-care centers); elementary schools, where children joined the *Pioneros* (Pioneers); *escuelas al campo* (schools in the countryside); and high schools, technical or vocational schools, and universities, which had their own mass organizations controlled by the Party. Outside school, the young were further inculcated with the values and ideals of a perfect communist through the mass media, directed by the Party and state and, if they qualified, through their membership in the Union of Young Communists (UJC).[2] Those who did not become UJC members still continued to be exposed to high dosages of political indoctrination through their participation in the Committees for the Defense of the Revolution (CDRs), the Federation of Cuban Women (FMC), the Confederation of Cuban Workers (CTC), the Revolutionary Armed Forces (FAR), and the Youth Labor Army. Hence, over the decades, the regime had good reason to believe that their high expectations of molding an elite corps of new men and women were in fact being realized.

However, the socialization process itself was another root cause for generational tensions. To be sure, socialization did produce legions of "good communist youth," particularly during the first three decades of the Revolution. But in time, according to Fernández, the agencies of state socialization themselves became "a check on reality" for those youths who had internalized the socializing agencies' idealistic goals, only to find them unfulfilled or violated by those same agencies. For example, Fernández (2004, Appendix B) cites one interviewee's account of the *escuela al campo*, in which youths came to view the schools in the countryside as *"un relajo, un choteo"*—a joke—where students did the least possible amount of agricultural work and partied as much as possible. This contradiction between high-minded idealism and actual experience produced not only dissonance but also disillusionment and cynicism among the young. Presumably, such a reaction became more prevalent once the heady days of the initial, romanticized era of the Revolution receded and youths became more and more exposed to the unvarnished realities of work and everyday life under totalitarian, bureaucratized rule.[3]

---

[2] By the early 1990s, Fernández (2004) notes, the UJC had almost 1.5 million members, or about 25 percent of all Cuban youth.

[3] Even as early as 1967, one of the authors (Gonzalez) encountered a young UJC leader on a state farm in central Cuba who, in guarded terms, expressed a surprising degree of cynicism regarding the work (or lack thereof) that was being accomplished by his youthful charges and the instructions being given by higher authorities.

A third root cause was the fact that the state and Party could not entirely monopolize the socialization process because the young were also being exposed to less-formalistic means of socialization by families and close friends. These small islands of personal, autonomous social space existed even during the period of totalitarianism, sometimes exposing youths to alternative views and norms of conduct.[4] With the mutation to post-totalitarianism that resulted from the collapse of the Soviet Union in 1991 and the economic crisis that followed, these islands of social space expanded as Party and state controls weakened. Youths became exposed to alternative, usually informal, venues of socialization through their networks of intimate friends, their participation in Catholic and protestant religious and lay organizations and Afro-Cuban sects, their contacts with political dissidents, their involvement with rock groups, and their artistic and intellectual circles, etc. As the 1990s wore on, the attitudes, norms, and behavior of more and more youths began to deviate from what the older generation of leaders wanted and had expected from the "children of the Revolution."

In the meantime, the dissonance, disillusionment, and cynicism setting in among youths were not sudden but, rather, gradual and cumulative, ultimately producing what Fernández calls "desocialization"—the rejection in varying degrees of the norms, dogmas, and goals prescribed by the regime. The process of desocialization was accelerated over time by a series of externally driven developments that began to shake the assumptions, beliefs, and values held by youths.

The first major accelerator was the return of some 100,000 exiles to the island on brief visits in 1978–1979, an event that suddenly gave the lie to the government's claim that the *gusanos* (worms) who

---

[4] With the advent of totalitarianism, Cubans came to rely on their *cara doble* to conceal their real feelings about the regime, thus making it difficult for foreign observers to gauge the extent of disillusionment among the youth. But in his 1968 visit to the island, one of the authors (Gonzalez) gained the confidence of three young men who had been close friends since school days. They expressed strong criticisms of the regime—although one hid his true feelings from his friends under his *cara doble*. Gonzalez' encounters with *"los muchachos"* served as the basis of two chapters—"Conflicts" and "La Cara Doble"—that appear in his novel, *Ernesto's Ghost* (2002b).

had fled to the United States had been living miserable existences under the exploitative yoke of capitalism. What Cubans on the island saw instead were returning relatives and friends flush with material wealth as evidenced by their cash, jewelry, and photos of privately owned homes, automobiles, and businesses. The influx of exiles, in turn, was a major factor that triggered the 1980 Mariel exodus; the young constituted 41 percent of the islanders who chose to depart for Florida.[5]

The next accelerator was the "Campaign to Rectify Errors and Negative Tendencies," which was launched in 1986. The "Rectification Campaign" called for greater state centralization and ideological orthodoxy at a time when Gorbachev was introducing liberalizing reforms in the U.S.S.R. under *perestroika* and *glasnost.* The fact that Cuba was reverting to heightened centralization and bureaucratic and ideological controls at the very moment that the Soviet Union was surging ahead in an attempt to humanize communism surely was not lost on some of Cuba's more observant, liberal-minded youth. In any event, Fernández (2004, Appendix B) observes that the effort by Roberto Robaina and other leaders of the Union of Young Communists to revitalize the UJC and win over youth through less-formalistic, more-flexible forms of socialism was contradicted by the Rectification Campaign.[6]

Another accelerator at the time was the slow growth of the economy during the decade of the 1980s, particularly after 1986, which began to limit the opportunities that youth had for future social advancement. The sluggish economy, coupled with the reversals in economic policy (from centralization to decentralization to limited liberalization in the late 1970s, then back to recentralization after 1986) also signified elite incompetence. Cuban socialism, in short,

---

[5] However, youths were underrepresented in the Mariel boatlift, because the 27-and-under age group made up 56 percent of the island's population. Also, many of the young may have had little choice but to accompany their parents. A more telling figure would be the percentage of those between 16 and 27 years of age.

[6] Although not an exogenous event, the Ochoa affair in summer 1989, in which Cuba's most-famous field general was executed following a show trial, may have also accelerated the disaffection of youth from the regime.

was not working, as evidenced by its failure to improve materially the lives of the Cuban people.

The major accelerator that sharpened the division between the older leadership and youth, of course, was the fall of communism, which began in 1989 in Eastern Europe and ended with the disappearance of the Soviet Union in 1991. This seismic event produced shock waves felt on the island during the 1990s, including among Cuban youth. Politically, the young now had more reason than ever to doubt the competence of the regime's top leadership. Ideologically, they could see that Cuba was virtually alone and struggling against the tide of history. Economically, and most disturbing of all, their own futures looked bleak. As Fernández (2004, Appendix B) notes, "The economic crisis shook the goodwill the regime still enjoyed among the youth as their hopes for a better tomorrow faded under the harsh light of today. '*Mañana*' was far away. . . . Even those who had played by the rules of the game found that their sacrifices had come to naught." Perhaps best capturing such anomie among Cuban youth was the statement commonly made to George Plinio Montalván during his 1997 visit: "*No creo en el comunismo, ni en el socialismo, ni en el capitalismo. Ahora creo en el yo-ismo.*" (I neither believe in communism, nor in socialism, nor in capitalism. I [only] believe in me-ism.)[7]

Hence, the regime's Special Period accelerated the widening distance between the state and youth as heightened austerity not only crushed personal aspirations and rendered accomplished skills useless but also contradicted the socialist and nationalist ideals that youths had absorbed. The government, for example, cut back on higher education, shifting the emphasis to technical and vocational schooling in hotel management, biotechnology, and agriculture—areas in which opportunities for employment were still to be found. But in the meantime, according to Fernández, youths accounted for an estimated 74 percent of the unemployed in the early 1990s—a repudiation of the Revolution's commitment to full employment and social

---

[7] September 5, 2003, note from George Plinio Montalván to the authors.

justice. Many young professionals found they could only survive and *"resolver"* (make do) by turning to hustling, prostitution, black-market activities, and self-employment—activities that made their high-level of education superfluous. Youths saw that those who received dollar remittances from abroad were far better off than those good Revolutionaries who lacked access to hard currency—a repudiation of the Revolution's commitment to social equity. And young (as well as older) Cubans found themselves barred from hotels, beaches, discotheques, restaurants, and special stores reserved exclusively for foreigners under the government's policy of apartheid tourism—a personal affront as well as a striking repudiation of the core nationalist values of the Revolution.

These and other disturbing developments quickened the process of desocialization that had been spreading among the young over the past decade or so. They now became increasingly aware and critical of the *doble moral* in which, as Fernández recounts, there exists a clash between public and private morality, between political rhetoric and everyday life, between purported goals and accomplishments and actual performance by the government.

Desocialization, in turn, became reflected in behavior. A significant, and increasingly visible, number of youths literally turned away from the regime's expected norms of conduct by embracing Western pop music, clothing, and fads, often engaging in explicit "anti-social" behavior, such as taking illicit drugs, stealing, and engaging in prostitution. According to Fernández, the young constituted about 75 percent of the *balseros* (rafters) who left the island in the early 1990s. Based on his analysis of the Cuban media at the end of the decade, he also calculates that possibly as many as 50 percent of the UJC members declined to join the Party when they became eligible for membership. A May 2001 article in the Party's official newspaper, *Granma,* thus severely criticized the work of the UJC, singling out its poor performance, lack of competent leadership, and high rates of absenteeism among members. Other articles in the media, Fernández notes, reported that 25 percent of the students in Havana province had a medical excuse not to attend schools in the country, while draft dodging was on the increase. Clearly, the regime was losing the battle

to create, in Fidel's words of March 1959, "a more marvelous generation . . . one that will truly be more perfect than us."

The Regime's Counteroffensive and Implications for the Future

Notwithstanding the fact that growing numbers of Cuban youth were
turning away from the government, nearly 1.5 million Cubans were
UJC members in the early 1990s and seemingly shared the ideals and
values of the Revolution and appeared willing to make the personal
sacrifices required of "good communist youth." These youths constitute the group that Fernández calls "the loyalists." Many have been
rewarded with favorable posts in the Party, state, and military estab-
lishments, and in the dollar economy. Hence, not only are they favored by the present status quo, but they also stand to gain after
Castro is gone because they are destined to assume positions of
greater power and privilege in a successor communist regime.

However, mirroring the rest of the population, most Cuban
youth are disaffected, but their disaffection is not homogenous; they
are split into two remaining camps—"the in-betweens" and "the opponents." The "in-between" youths, according to Fernández, are
characterized by more nuanced, ambiguous, and troubled attitudes
toward the government. Hit hard by the economic crisis after 1989,
they have had their expectations for employment, upward mobility,
and material well-being dashed. They want the continuation of the
welfare state in education and health, yet they also value individualism. Hence, they yearn for greater room for creative expression, and
they want greater economic liberalization in order to realize their material ambitions. They also want political reforms in order to obtain
authentic participation and greater self-efficacy in politics. But thus
far the "in-betweens" have been unable to articulate a clear political
alternative to the regime and they lack political organization.

The "opponents," Fernández notes, do not necessarily constitute
an organized political movement, although some have formed independent dissident organizations or joined established dissident and

human-rights groups. But by and large they are "a variegated and disconnected mass of *'jóvenes'*" who reject Cuban socialism through their legal or illegal behavior, whether civil or uncivil, ranging from attendance at religious services and adopting Western mores to participating in the informal or black-market economy and other illegal activities. Fernández believes that they are most likely to form the social basis for spontaneous mass riots of the type that occurred on the Malecón waterfront in August 1994.

Given the absence of survey data and the prevalence of the *cara doble*, it is impossible to determine the extent to which the group of "in-betweens" may in fact lean toward the first or third camp. Whatever the case may be, it was and remains incumbent for the regime to attract youths from this "in-between" group back into the loyalist camp or at the very least prevent them from moving into "the opponents" group. However, it is doubtful that the regime can achieve either objective under conditions of increased repression and more-difficult economic times.

Meanwhile, the regime has tried by various means to win the hearts and minds of the young. In the 1980s, it sought to revitalize the UJC under Roberto Robaina's energetic leadership, an effort that was largely undone by the Rectification Campaign and the downturn of the economy. With the advent of the Special Period of the 1990s, it sought to stem further youth alienation by authorizing rock concerts, allowing young musicians and other artists to travel abroad, refurbishing education centers, and establishing computer clubs. It also began infusing the PCC with younger members. Thus, at the Fourth Party Congress in December 1991, Castro declared that, "We injected a good dose of young blood into the recent Party Congress, because we are convinced that is essential and that there is a need for health and energy for the increasingly complex and tense function of the state" (*Foreign Broadcast Information Service,* Latin America, 1991, p. 1). The PCC website subsequently reported that the Party had enrolled 232,457 new members in the 1992–1996 period, presumably with the lion's share having been drawn from the UJC.

The regime also employed the Elián González affair in 2001 to mobilize the youth, along with the rest of the population, in a new nationalist crusade directed against the United States and especially the Miami exile community. Middle-school-age children in particular were mobilized for Elián marches and took part in meetings—*Tribunas Abiertas*—designed to instill greater nationalism and revolutionary fervor, and to better wage *La Gran Batalla de Ideas* (the Great Battle of Ideas). Since the Elián affair, Fernández reports, the regime has used not only nationalist appeals in its campaign to rally the young, but also humanistic ones by citing the threat globalization poses to Cuban society's sense of national identity, social justice, and Revolution.

Save for the "the loyalists," however, much of Cuba's youth today appears to have largely disengaged from political life. As Fernández observes, "decades of coerced participation in a hyperpoliticized environment" have led to widespread political exhaustion. This state of affairs diminishes the prospects that young Cubans will engage in collective political action against the regime, opting instead to pursue their private interests—material well-being, self-expression, spiritual contentment, etc. They may try to accomplish this pursuit on the island or by defecting abroad. Indeed, the defection of Cuba's leading pop star, Carlos Manuel, to the United States in June 2003 is emblematic of the depoliticization of Cuban youths and their inclination to flee rather than fight the regime.[8] Such a predisposition stands in striking contrast to the position taken by young *refuseniks* in the former Soviet Union, young Polish workers in Solidarity, and students in Prague, whose actions helped bring down communism.

Hence, if such behavior continues into the future, a successor communist regime could have an initial political advantage because it would most likely confront a low level of active, organized opposition among Cuba's youth. As is the case at present, politics will remain predominantly in the hands of the regime's more fervent supporters—including "the loyalists" among the young who are most versed

---

[8] The 30-year-old Manuel defected after his salsa band, Carlos Manuel and His Clan, had performed in Mexico City. Despite enjoying a relatively privileged life as Cuba's hottest musician, he said he chose to defect because of the government's heightened repression in recent months and the limits that Cuba's bureaucracy placed on his career. Romero (2003).

in politics and have a strong personal stake in perpetuating the present order.

However, unless reformers are able to gain control, a successor communist regime is certain to face the same problems in trying to reengage the young as have bedeviled the Castro regime for more than a decade. To win the hearts and minds of youth will require that the successor regime transform itself sufficiently to push through fundamental, liberalizing political and economic reforms. A more responsive political system would have to be introduced that, for example, gives the young basic political freedoms and a sense of real political self-efficacy, as well as more cultural freedom for self-expression. A new economic model would need to be pursued that provides for a more robust private sector and material rewards so that the young are given incentives to remain on the island and participate actively in its economic reconstruction. These, of course, are the kinds of policies that would more likely be adopted by a popularly elected democratic government.

The retreat from politics by Cuban youth also poses problems for a democratic transition in the post-Castro era. Although opposition to a successor communist regime may intensify, the regime's opponents will be severely handicapped if they are unable to mobilize the active support of the rest of society, especially the young. As Fernández notes, a society cannot create democratic institutions, norms, and practices without popular participation. It may well take the rise of a new generation before democracy can begin to take root on the island.

In the meantime, the more probable scenario after Castro is gone is one in which many of Cuba's youth who today constitute the "in-betweens" and "opponents" will try to leave the island in pursuit of a better life abroad. As both Fernández (2004) and McCarthy (2004) point out in their youth and demographic studies, respectively, a mass exodus by the young would be a serious blow to the island's economic recovery. It would reduce the numbers of young workers who are needed in the labor force not only to revitalize the economy but also to support social programs for both children and an increasingly aging population. Therefore, even if a successor communist regime is able to consolidate its political power, it, like a democratic successor, would probably face enormous economic problems caused in part by the disengagement of youths from Cuban socialism—either through their withdrawal as internal *emigres* via their choice of personal lifestyles or their physical departure from the island.

CHAPTER FOUR

Cuba's Racial Divide[1]

Background

During its first 30 years in power, the Castro government made impressive strides in promoting racial equality, in the process building a reservoir of political capital for the regime—especially for "Fidel" personally—among Afro-Cubans. To outside admirers and observers, Cuba appeared to have become a "raceless society."

However, racial prejudice and discrimination were not entirely erased from the Cuban psyche. Racial tensions resurfaced in the 1990s with the advent of the Special Period, because Afro-Cubans, defined as blacks and mulattos—especially blacks—were hardest hit by the crisis. Blacks and mulattos thus figured predominantly in the riots on the Malecón on the Havana waterfront in August 1994. Increased migration from the impoverished, blacker eastern half of the island to Havana starting in the early 1990s was accompanied by a surge in crime and prostitution—and a white backlash and strong government reaction. The April 2003 summary execution of three young blacks after they tried to hijack a ferryboat fueled charges of racism by the regime's critics on the island and abroad—charges that gained some credibility owing to the regime's predominantly white leadership.

---

[1] This chapter draws in part upon UCLA political science professor Mark Q. Sawyer's unpublished paper, "Race and the Future of Cuba," and other sources as noted.

This analysis delves into the reasons for the racial question coming back to haunt the Castro regime despite the gains it made in promoting racial equality. It then explores the implications of Cuba's looming racial divide for the post-Castro era. In the process, four major points will be developed:

- For three decades, Afro-Cuban support for the regime and for Fidel Castro personally stemmed largely from the opportunities for social mobility that were created with the huge expansion of the state apparatus and public sector of the economy.
- This reservoir of Afro-Cuban political support has been depleted during the past decade, because the negative effects of the Special Period have hurt blacks more than whites. Afro-Cubans, particularly blacks, have also benefited less than whites from the new market economy and have felt the sting of heightened racial discrimination.
- What goodwill and trust the present regime still enjoys among Afro-Cubans is unlikely to carry over to a communist successor regime after Fidel is gone, unless that regime is better able to satisfy their aspirations—a feat that is now made less likely owing to the island's deteriorating economic situation.
- Existing racial cleavages and attitudinal differences between Afro-Cubans and whites are likely to deepen in the future and overlap religious, economic, and regional divisions. Such divisions will make it more difficult for a civil society to form and for government to enact market reforms and develop the eastern half of the island.

Before elaborating on these points, we must first note the methodological and other problems that characterize research on race in contemporary Cuba.

The Elusive Subject of Race in Castro's Cuba

Empirical data on questions of race, racism, and racial attitudes in contemporary Cuba are incomplete. When they do exist, the data are often contradictory. The last national census in which racial data were collected was in 1981—in itself a revealing omission that suggests that the government has since sought to replace racial identity with national identity. Blacks and mulattos made up 34 percent of the population in the 1981 census, compared with 26 percent in the 1970 census and 26.9 percent in the 1953 census. The 1970-to-1981 increase in the percentage of Afro-Cubans reflected the effects of out-migration by whites and the high birthrates of Afro-Cubans after 1959. Because racial identity is a subjective concept, and Cubans of all color tend to denigrate blackness, the 34-percent figure in 1981 may have understated the actual percentage of Afro-Cubans. On the other hand, the widely cited Central Intelligence Agency (CIA) estimates of 11 percent black and 51 percent mulatto for Cuba in the 1990s could well be on the high side (Central Intelligence Agency, 2002). According to an uncorroborated report filed by an independent Cuban journalist in late 2002, Cuba's Center for Anthropology estimated that 10 percent of the population was black and 30 percent was mulatto, although the Center acknowledged that there well could be subjective variations within each group (Márquez Linares, 2002). Given these discrepant estimates, this study assumes that Afro-Cubans currently constitute somewhere close to 50 percent of the island's 11.2 million inhabitants.

The prevailing atmosphere of societal mistrust and state repression that continue in Cuba make pinpointing contemporary racial attitudes on the part of both whites and Afro-Cubans difficult. As a result, the few attitudinal surveys taken by visiting American and other foreign scholars have relied on small, informal, and nonrandomized samples, which at best give only a glimpse of the actual racial and race-based attitudes held by respondents. Whether the attitudes reflected in these studies are representative of the rest of the population is open to question. In any case, much of the literature on contemporary race issues in Cuba relies on impressionistic observations and anecdotal evidence rather than on verifiable empirical data, and it often fails to differentiate between blacks and mulattos. As will be discussed later in this chapter, the latter differentiation problem becomes even more complicated because blacks and mulattos are further differentiated according to their hair, shades of skin color, eye color, and African features, with "blacks" generally tending to experience the most discrimination. Hence, due to the limitation of contemporary data on race in Cuba, much of the analysis that follows is necessarily inferential.

Race in Pre- and Post-1959 Cuba

Cuba's sugar-plantation economy required the importation of African slaves during the Spanish colonial period. The resulting black and emerging mulatto populations remained poor, largely uneducated, and heavily concentrated in the easternmost province of Oriente—the island's most important sugar-growing area, which in 1976 was subdivided into five provinces (Guantánamo, Santiago de Cuba, Granma, Holguín, Las Tunas). Although slavery was not abolished by Spain until 1886, more than 20 years after Lincoln's Emancipation Proclamation, Cuban racism nevertheless appeared to be more "humanized" when compared with the overt, violent racism found in the United States.[2] The Spanish colonial government, for example, barred discrimination in public job hiring as early as 1887; two years later, racial discrimination was prohibited in theaters, bars, and restaurants, and schools were opened to black children.

Nonetheless, Afro-Cubans felt sufficiently impoverished and oppressed to become *mambises* (freedom fighters) during the War of Independence (1895–1898), in which they fought both for the island's liberation from Spain and the promise of racial equality in a

---

[2] In "Masking Hispanic Racism: A Cuban Case Study," May 1999, pp. 57–74 (posted on the Afro-Cuba Web), Miguel A. de la Torre argues that the comparison with the United States is superficial, because it ignores that under both colonial rule and the Republic, Cuba had less obvious but nonetheless institutionalized forms of discrimination and oppression.

new, more colorblind society. The war in fact provided them with new opportunities for social mobility, power, and recognition, as exemplified by Cuba's most famous and beloved field general—the mulatto Antonio Maceo, who was killed in battle in 1896. But racism returned under the American occupation of 1898–1902 as black veterans were excluded from public administration, the police, and the Rural Guard.

Racism was not confined to American authorities, however; it flourished following the establishment of the Republic in 1902. Despite the end of slavery, some plantation owners still thought "they owned the blacks" (Montejo, 1968, p. 96), who in any case were mostly hired only during the peak sugar season (December–May). What little existed of the black peasantry was dispossessed, with former small black landholders entering the rural proletariat or migrating to the cities in search of work. In 1907, politically aspiring but displaced Afro-Cuban veterans, who had represented the small, emerging black middle class before the war, formed their own political party—*El Partido Independiente de Color* (The Independent Party of Color)—to press for racial equality, jobs, and a share of political power. But three years later the Liberal government prohibited parties that were organized on the basis of race, after which blacks rose up in open revolt in the "race war" of 1912. Thousands of blacks were massacred in that rebellion, and the savagery of the white repression in some cases equaled that of the lynchings in the Deep South in the first decades of the 20th century.[3]

Afro-Cubans did not challenge the established social, economic, and political order during the remainder of the period of the Republic. Instead, most worked within the political system, which allowed them their own social, religious, and cultural clubs, and mutual-aid societies. Some blacks and mulattos rose to considerable prominence. Thus, Sergeant-Stenographer Fulgencio Batista, of mixed Afro-

---

[3] Many black rebel captives were hung from lampposts by their genitals after false reports that white women had been raped. De la Torre (1999) and Casal (1989) have cited these incidents as evidence of the white man's fear that black sexuality threatened white civilization.

Cuban-Chinese origins, led the "Sergeants' Revolt" of 1933, became Cuba's de facto ruler for the next seven years, was elected president in 1940, and seized power in 1952 by means of a military coup. There were five Afro-Cuban Senators out of 54 in 1945, and 12 representatives out of 127 in the lower chamber. Organized labor had black and mulatto leaders, and Afro-Cubans made up 14.5 percent of professionals in 1943.

Nonetheless, color and lower-class status tended to correlate: Afro-Cubans accounted for 46.9 percent of domestic and personal-service personnel, 44.2 percent of construction, and 39.7 percent of recreation and entertainment in the 1943 census. According to historian Louis A. Pérez (1988, p. 307), Afro-Cubans occupied the lower rungs of the socioeconomic ladder prior to 1959:

> Almost 30 percent of the population of color over twenty years of age was illiterate. Blacks tended to constitute a majority in the crowded tenement buildings of Havana. They suffered greater job insecurity, more underemployment/unemployment, poorer health care, and constituted a proportionately larger part of the prison population. They generally earned lower wages than whites, even in the same industries. Afro-Cubans were subjected to systematic discrimination, barred from hotels, resorts, clubs, and restaurants.

Institutionalized racism was probably less prevalent than personal discrimination, which was summed up by the Cuban racial proverb, *"Juntos pero no revueltos; cada cosa en su lugar"* (Together but not scrambled; everything in its place).[4] That proverb and, with it, the old order, would be overturned by the 1959 Revolution.

Led by middle- and upper-middle-class leaders, the Rebel Army that triumphed over the Batista regime was predominantly white in composition. Major Juan Almeida and, later, the communist leader

---

[4] Quoted in de la Torre (1999).

Blas Roca, were the most notable exceptions in the new regime.[5] Despite the paucity of Afro-Cubans in its ranks, the Revolutionary government announced an end to legal race discrimination in March 1959, which opened up all-white clubs and beaches to all Cubans.

More important than this symbolic act was the government's commitment to full equality and to improving the living standards of the urban and rural lower classes. As Jorge I. Domínguez (1978, p. 225) observes, "Because blacks were disproportionately represented among the poor, they were likely to benefit disproportionately from any improvement in the lot of the poor." Through its radical redistributive policies, including slashing rents and utility rates, raising wages, enacting agrarian reform, and redistributing houses and apartments vacated by departing upper- and middle-class Cubans, the government solidified its support among the poor and disadvantaged. Hence, Afro-Cubans became the most fervent supporters of the Revolution, as evidenced by a 1962 survey that showed that 80 percent of black industrial workers were favorable to the Revolution compared with 67 percent of the white workers (Zeitlin, 1970, p. 77).

The large waves of out-migration by disaffected whites in the initial post-1959 period, then again in the mid-1960s and in 1980, created an occupational vacuum and opened up houses and apartments, which Afro-Cubans now filled. As Alejandro de la Fuente points out (1998, p. 2), "Upward mobility was achieved without the social tensions which are generated by competition for scarce resources and lucrative employment. Through the 1970s, the need for professionals, technicians, and qualified workers was greater than their availability." Moreover, by taking race out of the equation and framing its social policies in terms of class, and by ascribing racism to imperialism, capitalism, and the pre-1959 white elite, the government minimized racial tensions and a white backlash (de la Fuente, 1998, p.2):

---

[5] Almeida, in particular, became the one black leader who would feature prominently in the high councils of government and Party in the decades that followed, including to this day.

> Manifestations of racism became socially unacceptable: They were both anti-revolutionary and counter-revolutionary. Race itself disappeared from public political discourse. . . . Revolutionary Cuba was envisioned as a raceless society, one in which the color of one's skin would have no influence on one's opportunities.[6]

And in fact, Cuba achieved significant, measurable progress in reducing racial inequality.

In 1981, according to de la Fuente, life expectancy in Cuba matched that of the developed countries and Afro-Cuban longevity lagged by only one year the longevity of the white population. There was also near parity between races in education: 11.2 percent of the black population and 9.6 percent of mulatto population over 25 years of age had high school diplomas compared with 9.9 percent among the white population. College graduation by blacks (3.5 percent) and mulattos (3.2 percent) for the 25-year-and-over population was also only slightly behind whites (4.4 percent). In terms of occupational mobility, blacks and mulattos held 22.1 and 22.9 percent of the professional jobs, respectively, compared with 22.2 percent for whites in 1981. However, a 1987 occupational census revealed that blacks and mulattos—who comprised a 34-percent share of the total population in the 1981 census—were underrepresented in government: They held 27 percent of government management positions at the national, provincial, and local levels compared with 72.5 percent for whites (de la Fuente, 1998, pp. 2–3). Still, Afro-Cubans had clearly made impressive advances toward equality as measured by health, education, and social indicators.

What Afro-Cubans lost under the Castro regime was their former ability to form independent race-based associations with which to express their identity and advance their interests. First, the Revolutionary state and then the totalitarian state imposed a highly centralized political order, in which there was only one political party. Cuba's once pluralistic, multiracial society was replaced by a society

---

[6] As noted earlier, these figures should be treated with some degree of caution, owing to the somewhat problematic nature of racial statistics in Cuba, including the 1981 census.

emphasizing national unity, a society without race and without class. Hence, there was no place for racial distinctions and preferences, much less for organized racial politics. The government even closely monitored religious activities by Afro-Cuban sects. Still, the government played the race card to its advantage, domestically as well as internationally. At every opportunity, it condemned racism in the United States and other Western countries, forged close diplomatic and political ties to Africa, and dispatched combat troops to Angola to repel the forces of South Africa's apartheid regime.[7] The international success of Cuba's baseball, boxing, and track teams, which were predominantly Afro-Cuban and which won scores of medals at the Olympic and Pan American Games in the 1970s and 1980s, gave blacks and mulattos further cause for supporting the government.[8]

Inequalities remained, however. Through the 1980s, the most-dilapidated areas in the cities tended to be disproportionately occupied by blacks and mulattos, according to de la Fuente. The rate of increase in criminal activity in 1981–1985, he reports, was substantially higher in the easternmost provinces, which had the largest percentage of blacks and mulattos. Blacks and mulattos were overrepresented in the prison population in the late 1980s, accounting for 80 percent of the prisoners in the *Combinado del Este* prison outside Havana. They also represented 72 percent of the 643 socially dangerous cases brought to trial in Havana in December 1986, of which 345 were black and 120 were mulatto (de la Fuente, 1998, p. 5).[9]

---

[7] The use of Cuba's foreign policy toward Africa to deflect attention away from the lack of Afro-Cubans' political power at home is the underlying theme in Moore (1988).

[8] In recent years, however, the much-publicized defections by Afro-Cuban star athletes, especially in baseball, have hurt the government's image at home and abroad.

[9] The government blames the high number of Afro-Cuban prisoners and delinquents on the fact that Afro-Cubans still represent the poorest stratum of society.

Increased Racial Tensions with the Advent of the Special Period

The economic edifice upon which Cuba's social compact had been erected, and which had made possible Cuba's gains in racial equality, nearly collapsed with the crisis of the 1990s. Whipsawed by both the economic crisis itself *and* the measures taken to ameliorate the crisis during the Special Period, Afro-Cubans—especially blacks—became most vulnerable and suffered disproportionately more than did white Cubans. No longer did loyalty and support for the Revolution, the government, and Fidel seem to matter for the increasingly disadvantaged blacks and mulattos. For a brief day, on August 5, 1994, the combustible mixture of frustration, sense of betrayal, and rage over their plight exploded on the Havana waterfront as thousands, with Afro-Cubans reportedly in the majority, rioted before the regime's security forces restored order.

The social mobility achieved by Afro-Cubans had been facilitated by the enormous expansion of the state sector under the Castro regime. Afro-Cubans secured positions as skilled workers, teachers, doctors, technicians, bureaucrats, and administrators in state agencies, schools, hospitals, and enterprises. The modest peso-dominated incomes they earned were sufficient as long as the socialist economy, propped up by Soviet subsidies, continued to provide housing, food, commodities, health, and other social services gratis or at low cost. But once the economy nose-dived and acute shortages developed, their state salaries and wages became grossly inadequate to pay for the goods and services that were only available on the black market. In the meantime, state agencies and enterprises began to be eliminated, downsized, or idled in order to cut mounting budget deficits, causing unemployment and underemployment. Up to this point, Cubans of all colors suffered more or less equally under the acute austerity of the Special Period.

As de la Fuente points out, what made the economic crisis even worse for blacks and mulattos were the "racially differentiated effects" of some of the reforms introduced by the government, beginning with the dollarization of the economy in mid-1993. The legalized holding of dollars, said de la Fuente, "tended to fragment Cuban society along the lines of those who have them and who do not." Family remittances, which totaled $600–$800 million per year and became one of the three major sources of dollars, were less available for Afro-Cubans: According to the 1990 U.S. Census, 83.5 percent of Cuban-Americans identified themselves as white. For example, de la Fuente (1998, p. 6), calculates that whites received the lion's share of the remittances—upwards of $680 million out of the total of $800 million. These dollar remittances were used to purchase scarce commodities, automobiles, and better housing, or to set up *paladares* and other micro-enterprises with which to earn additional dollars. The net effect of the dollarization reform was to suddenly widen the gap in incomes and living standards between whites and Afro-Cubans in a society that had been socialized in the norms and expectations of social equality.

Another major source of dollar accumulation is work in the tourist industry, to which the government now assigned highest priority as a way of bolstering much-needed foreign earnings. But blacks, in particular, were left out of this especially lucrative sector of Cuba's emerging market economy because of persistent racial discrimination among whites and even lighter-skinned mulattos toward blacks. This subject deserves a note of explanation.

There is still a tendency among Cubans today—including among blacks themselves—to denigrate blackness while prizing straight hair, lightness of skin, and less-negroid features. Blacks and mulattos are categorized by whether they have straight or wavy hair (preferred) or kinky hair (less desirable). Then, there are no less than nine permutations among blacks and mulattos, based on skin color and other features, ranging from the most desirable, *leche con una gota de café* (milk with a drop of coffee) to the least desirable, *negro azul y trompido* (blue black with thick lips). The influx of white foreign tourists in pursuit of sex has further reinforced the perception that straight or wavy hair and lighter skin are best.[10]

---

[10] For all the permutations currently used by Cubans, and the racial types most favored by tourists, see Tattlin (2002, p. 88).

As a result, blacks have found it difficult to find employment in the tourist sector. Forty percent of respondents in a survey conducted by de la Fuente and a co-investigator in Havana and Santiago de Cuba in 1994 agreed that blacks were denied the same opportunities as whites in the tourist industry. According to one of their respondents, a white female manager in Santiago (de la Fuente, 1998, pp. 6–7),

> . . . [T]here is a lot racial prejudice in the tourist sector. . . . In my corporation, for instance, out of 500 workers there are only five blacks. . . . There is no explicit policy stating that one has to be white to work in tourism, but it is regulated that people must have a pleasant appearance [*aspecto agradable*] and blacks do not have it.[11]

A more recent study by Cuba's Center for Anthropology reported that whites accounted for 80 percent of the personnel in the tourist industry, compared with 5 percent for blacks (Márquez Linares, 2002).[12]

Cuba's small private farms and cooperatives are a third source of dollar earnings. After delivering their assigned quotas to the state, farmers are able to sell their agricultural surplus at free-market prices in the farmers' markets, which were reintroduced in September 1994 to stem worsening food shortages. But as noted earlier, the black peasantry was largely displaced in the first decades of the Republic, with the result that Afro-Cubans do not benefit from this reform. Indeed, a survey conducted by the University of Havana in 1992 revealed that whites represented 98 percent of Cuba's private farmers and 95 percent of the members of the agricultural cooperatives (de la Fuente, 1998, p. 7).

Since the early 1990s, therefore, blacks have become the most-disadvantaged group in Cuba's racial hierarchy. According to data

---

[11] The takeover of tourist hotels and resorts by Spanish and other foreign firms may in some cases inject a further element of racism in hiring employees.

[12] Mulattos presumably accounted for the remaining 15 percent of those employed in the tourist industry.

compiled by Mark Q. Sawyer, 15.4 percent of blacks had a lower level of education in 2000 than 6.1 percent of "middles" (less dark, or mulatto) and 3.6 percent of whites. Hence, they are "more likely to work as a laborer or be unemployed compared to any other group" (unpublished, p. 11). Stuck in low-paying menial or traditional state-sector jobs and left out of the new market economy, more and more Afro-Cubans were thus consigned to poverty.

The economic situation facing Afro-Cubans was bleakest in the eastern provinces, which are predominantly black and mulatto, and where there are fewer tourist facilities and joint ventures by foreign capital—major sources of employment opportunity. This situation produced an uncontrolled internal migration to Havana by so-called *palestinos*—literally Palestinians, but referring to darker-skinned migrants from the eastern provinces. Some 50,000 people migrated to Havana in 1996 according to one estimate, and, in fact, 92,000 people attempted to legalize their presence in Havana by the spring of 1997. The government responded by banning all further immigration to the city, fining illegal migrants and those housing them and ordering the deportation of illegal migrants to their place of origin (de la Fuente, 1998, p. 10).

In the meantime, racial prejudice intensified as Havana experienced a steep increase in violence, petty crimes, and prostitution, which white *Habaneros* attributed to the influx of *palestinos* and their delinquent ways. A white male professional complained to de la Fuente, for example, that "what blacks do is resort to robbery." According to another white interviewee, Fidel himself had stirred resentment among blacks by remarking, "'Habana Vieja [old Havana] is full of delinquents from Oriente'" (de la Fuente, 1998, p. 10).

In his attitudinal survey of Cubans of all colors in 2000, Sawyer also found that "whites are more likely to hold explicit racist attitudes towards blacks and to believe an array of negative stereotypes. . . . They are thus more likely to believe that blacks are more likely to be delinquents." For their part, blacks were more likely "to believe that they are treated unequally by police, and in public accommodations like discos . . . and to believe that they suffer from overt racial discrimination and that something must be done to alleviate the negative effects of discrimination" (Sawyer, unpublished, pp. 14–15).

In fact, although a breakdown of black and mulatto inmates is not available, Afro-Cubans remain overrepresented in the prison population. At the end of 2002, 70 percent of the prison population was either black or mulatto, according to an independent Cuban journalist Márquez Linares (2002).[13] The Cuba Transition Project at the University of Miami puts the figure even higher, claiming that Afro-Cubans under the age of 35 make up 85 percent of the prison population (2003a, p. 3). Prominent Afro-Cuban dissidents have been among those incarcerated, most recently Dr. Oscar Elias Biscet, a black physician who was released from prison in November 2002 after serving a three-year term. A practitioner of peaceful civil disobedience, but a harsh critic of the regime and its alleged racism, he was sentenced to another 25-year prison term in April 2003, following the arrest of 75 dissidents, human-rights activists, and independent journalists in March 2003.

If Afro-Cubans are overrepresented in the prison population, the opposite is generally true with respect to their representation in many of the key organs of political power. According to the Cuba Transition Project, Afro-Cubans occupy 33 percent of the seats in the National Assembly of People's Power, and make up nine of the 31 members (29 percent) of the Council of State. The latter is the more significant body; the National Assembly wields little political power, since it meets only twice a year for two days, and its role is confined to ratifying the laws and decrees issued by the Council of State. In the case of other, more-powerful institutions, Afro-Cuban representation drops considerably:

- Two Ministers of the 40-member Council of Ministers
- Three of the 15 provincial First Secretaries of the Communist Party of Cuba

---

[13] Márquez Linares' figure refers to the total prison population, as opposed to the figures for the Combinado del Este prison population and the category of "socially dangerous cases" in the late 1980s that were cited earlier in the section "Race in Pre- and Post-1959 Cuba."

- None of the 15 Presidents of the Provincial Assemblies of People's Power
- None of the 10 top Generals/senior posts in the Revolutionary Armed Forces (Cuba Transition Project, 2003a, p. 3)
- Five of the 24-member Political Bureau of the Communist Party of Cuba.[14]

In sum, a predominantly white leadership continues to lead Cuba's racially mixed society.

The Racial Divide and Its Implications for a Cuba After Castro

A case can be made that too much can be made of the racial divide in Cuba. The racial tensions that do exist, it could be argued, have been manageable, as evidenced by the fact that there has been no repeat during the past nine years of the riots that rocked the Havana waterfront in August 1994. It is also unclear to what extent racial discrimination affects all Afro-Cubans. To be sure, both anecdotal and statistical data show that blacks in particular are at the bottom of the racial hierarchy with respect to education, employment, political office, and incarceration. But less clear is whether mulattos experience the consequences of white prejudice anywhere near the same degree as blacks do. If they suffer less discrimination, there could well be a mulatto-black divide within the Afro-Cuban population itself, which may serve to defuse racial tensions, not only under the Castro regime but also under a future successor regime as well.

However, the above arguments tend to minimize the extent to which the existing cleavage between Afro-Cubans and whites is likely to intensify, as well as the extent to which it tends to overlap and reinforce other societal cleavages.

---

[14] The figure of five is based on photographs of the Political Bureau members that are on the Internet. See cubapolidata.com.

Certainly, the very presence of "Fidel" has thus far helped keep racial tensions manageable. Based on his interviews, Sawyer notes that it has been Castro's "personal credibility" that has enabled his regime to maintain black support despite the Special Period. However, Sawyer suggests that such support may not carry over into the future after Castro is gone (unpublished, p. 17):

> . . . [T]here appears to be a perception of growing inequality and black skepticism about economic trans-formations. While Castro lives, this skepticism and complaint are perhaps counterbalanced by the sym-bols of the revolution. But it may be difficult to trans-fer this [personal] trust to a new regime or a successor regime.

Indeed, Castro's personal appearance near the end of the riots on the Malecón in August 1994 may have helped to defuse the vola-tile situation, enabling his security forces to restore public order with-out having to fire on the protesters.

Besides the effectiveness of the regime's security apparatus, the economy's modest recovery starting in 1996 may have also prevented the recurrence of widespread unrest by Afro-Cubans. However, since 2002, the sugar industry has been undergoing a major downsizing, the effects of which are likely to be felt most among blacks, since they constitute a major portion of the industry's labor force. In the mean-time, the economic recovery is once again slowing down, with little growth expected for 2003 and probably 2004—a development that will worsen living conditions for all Cubans, but for Afro-Cubans most of all. Once again, therefore, the Castro regime may have to deal with heightened racial tensions, which could well carry over to the successor regime if they are not defused before Castro departs the scene.

Finally, while there may well be a racial divide among Afro-Cubans based on lighter versus darker skin color, the very existence of such a divide is likely to further intensify cleavages within the Cuban polity. For example, if either the current regime or its successor were to ignore the grievances of the black minority, who may make up only 10 to 11 percent of the population, and actively court the much larger mulatto population instead, such a strategy would surely prove racially divisive. Blacks would view it as a cynical attempt by the regime to align the interests of the white and mulatto population against those of the minority black population, thus institutionalizing discrimination against blacks, deepening the division between blacks on the one hand and mulattos and whites on the other, and erasing Cuba's image as a "raceless society." It would, in short, leave the issue of race to fester and perhaps explode at some future date.

Even if the present regime or successor regime eschews playing mulattos against blacks, race is still likely to remain a divisive issue for the Cuban polity: The issue of race touches on religion, economic systems, and regionalism. This overlap could well deepen divisions within the population, making more difficult the emergence of a civil society in a post-Castro Cuba while also complicating the public policy choices facing the government.

Sawyer, for example, found that nearly 60 percent of Afro-Cubans identify their religion as "Afro-Cuban," meaning *santería* and other syncretic religious faiths fusing Afro-Cuban beliefs with Catholicism, compared with only 22 percent who identified themselves as Catholic. Forty-six percent of whites, on the other hand, listed themselves as Catholic, whereas 17 percent identified themselves with an Afro-Cuban religion and 6.4 percent identified themselves as protestant.[15] Thus, there is a religious divide among Cubans that roughly parallels the racial divide between the white and Afro-Cuban population. The cleavage between those belonging to *santería* and other Afro-Cuban syncretic sects and those hewing to Catholicism may be made deeper by the Catholic Church's condemnation of Afro-Cuban religious practices as being heathen. In any event, these overlapping racial and religious divisions are likely to impede the future formation of a robust civil society able to constrain the state under a communist

---

[15] Those listing themselves as aetheist were 29.5 percent for whites, 23.9 percent for "middles," and 17.2 percent for blacks (Sawyer, unpublished, p. 14).

successor regime or shore up liberal democracy were an elected, democratic government to come to power.

A second divisive issue pertains to Cuba's economic strategy. Sawyer (unpublished, p. 16) found significant differences among racial groups concerning acceptance of the new economy:

> As one gets darker on the racial spectrum in Cuba, one is more likely to believe that some people benefit too much from private business and that there should be greater control over foreign investment. This is a strong rebuke to the current direction of the Cuban economy and the potential for market-based incentives.

Hence, whatever its ideological character, a successor regime is likely to encounter resistance to the enactment of deeper, liberalizing reforms that would open up the economy to private capital, entrepreneurial initiative, and foreign investors from the Afro-Cuban population, especially among older, more disadvantaged blacks.

Finally, any government that follows Castro will inherit the problem of uneven regional development. The eastern half of the island is poorer and less developed than the western half of Cuba. Havana and its environs are still the most economically developed region. As noted earlier in this chapter, the rural eastern provinces also have the heaviest concentrations of blacks and mulattos and were the principal sources of migration by so-called *palestinos* to metropolitan Havana and neighboring Matanzas province during the 1990s. The latest downturn in the economy could thus trigger renewed internal migration to Havana and other cities, with the concomitant prospect of racial tensions again intensifying.

The only permanent way to stem the flow of migrants from the east, of course, is to embark upon a plan for regional development that would generate increased opportunities for employment in the eastern provinces. But such a course would require the government in power to make some tough public policy choices when it is constrained by lack of sufficient resources and faced with competing social and economic priorities—among them, education, public health, retirement pensions, and infrastructure development for the entire island. For the government to opt for the development of the eastern region could provoke a white (and possibly mulatto) backlash if such a policy is perceived as being carried out at the expense of the rest of the population.

Similarly, the government might have to choose between developing the east, with its less-educated and less-skilled black population, and electing more cost-effective alternatives in other parts of the island that would offer better prospects for generating employment and foreign-exchange earnings. Moreover, to spur regional development, the government would probably have to invite foreign investors in. But it is by no means certain that such investors will be attracted to the eastern half of the island, unless it already offers economic opportunities and physical infrastructure, a trainable workforce, and a favorable political climate. Indeed, the antipathy toward private enterprise and foreign investments that Sawyer detected among the Afro-Cuban population could present an obstacle to the development of the eastern provinces.

The race issue, however, may in the end prove not only manageable but also resolvable if more Afro-Cubans can break the glass ceiling and ascend to positions of greater influence in the economy and polity. Here, blacks and mulattos could be aided by their numbers. That Afro-Cubans taken together make up close to half the island's population should give black and mulatto representatives political clout with which to press for greater racial equality in business and government. Hence, what kind of political system is in place could well determine the extent to which Afro-Cubans can achieve real gains in a post-Castro Cuba.

In this regard, on the one hand, a communist successor regime might appoint more Afro-Cubans to the upper echelons of the Party and state, for cosmetic purposes, without upsetting the balance of political power within the regime. On the other hand, an elected democratic government could provide Afro-Cubans with greater opportunities for advancement, because the system should enable them to optimize their political influence by means of the ballot box. The downside, of course, is that a more representative government in Cuba would need to be responsive to the demands of the populace if it is to survive. Hence, somehow it would have to find the resources and the political will to begin the development of the eastern provinces and satisfy the other needs of its Afro-Cuban supporters.

Even under the best of circumstances, the situation could well become more complicated politically if increased racial strains follow from an influx of white Cuban exiles during or following a democratic transition. In this respect, the attitudes and behavior of returning whites would certainly be critical variables of whether or not racial animosities intensified. However, for Afro-Cubans just to perceive and expect that they were once again about to become disadvantaged economically, socially, and politically because of the return of white exiles could also be just as important to whether the racial divide deepens or is surmounted.

Part II:
The Structural Challenges Ahead

The disaffection of Cuba's youth, the growing racial divide, and the population's more general disillusionment with the Revolution and even with Castro himself have been exacerbated by the economic crisis that began with the loss of Soviet economic aid. Castro's halt to the modest economic reforms that appeared to be pulling Cuba's economy out of the depth of the collapse has subsequently prolonged Cuba's economic troubles. However, even were Fidel (or his successors) to reverse Cuba's current economic policies, both the social welfare programs that were once the pride of the regime and the Cuban economy would still require major readjustments. The source of this predicament lies in the series of profound structural challenges that Cuba must address. These structural challenges include

- adjusting to an aging population
- coping with the legacy of an inflexible centralized economy
- realigning an industrial structure still dependent upon an outmoded and inefficient sugar industry.

How the government deals with these challenges will play a critical role in determining the island's longer-term economic future. The longer Cuba's leaders delay addressing these issues, the fewer degrees of freedom they will have at their disposal to do so and the more internal resistance they are likely to face in implementing the necessary adjustments.

As Pérez-López (see Appendix D) points out, Cuba has a long history of providing social services to its citizenry. However, the social service systems had glaring gaps in the access they provided to the island's residents. The Castro regime expanded this system dramatically by introducing a broad-based public pension system, providing access to free health care and education, and supplying a widespread system of housing and food subsidies that kept prices low and thus compensated for low wages. In addition to expanding the range of public services available, the regime also broadened access to these services, particularly to such groups as rural residents and Afro-Cubans, which previously had limited access to social services.

The resultant social service system has been one of the Castro regime's major accomplishments. It produced dramatic improvements in a variety of areas, including expanded literacy and school enrollment, higher levels of educational achievement, longer life expectancy and reduced morbidity and child mortality, guaranteed retirement incomes, and lower retirement ages. Indeed, it formed the implicit basis of the Cuban social compact, in which the regime provided the population with a broad array of benefits in implicit exchange for limited political freedom. The internal success of this social compact is reflected in the continued support Cuban émigrés express for keeping the achievements of the Revolution in the social services area (see Appendix D).

These achievements came at a cost, however. During the 1960s and 1970s, the Cuban government was spending more than one-third of its national budget on social expenditures—a figure that climbed to more than 40 percent during the 1980s and peaked at 46 percent in 1988. Because Cuba's economic growth during this period was modest (averaging between 3 and 4 percent per year), this expansion in social expenditures was possible in large part because of the influx of economic aid from the Soviet Union and the other Council of Mutual Economic Assistance (CMEA) states. At its peak, Soviet bloc trade and assistance constituted over 20 percent of Cuba's GDP.

With the dissolution of the Soviet Union and the cutoff of Soviet aid, the Cuban economy went into a tailspin: Real GDP declined by one-third between 1989 and 1993. Initially (1990 to 1993), the Cuban government attempted to protect its social-welfare programs through a program of massive state subsidies (Hernández-Cata,

2000). But the soaring state deficits and the rapid inflation that this policy engendered eventually (post-1993) led the Castro regime to severely cut back social programs. The net result has been a decline in service levels in virtually all categories of social programs (Mesa-Lago, 2000).

Overall per-capita expenditures on social services, for example, declined by 40 percent. Secondary-school enrollments dropped 10 percent, and higher education enrollments by more than 50 percent (Mesa-Lago, 2002). Morbidity rates increased for several categories of contagious disease, and maternal mortality rates more than doubled. The real value of pensions declined by 42 percent, and food subsidies and rationing were cut back, exacerbating the effects of declining pension values and reducing the daily intake of calories and proteins below minimum levels.

Although these cutbacks have had a profound effect on the living standards of the Cuban population, that effect has been uneven and, thus, even more insidious. Although social services in Cuba are provided to all regardless of their income, the expansion of Cuba's social safety net was particularly important in raising the living standards of Cuba's poor, particularly those living in rural areas and Afro-Cubans. The collapse of that safety net, together with the policies the regime introduced to counter the economic collapse, has reversed many of those gains. Rural residents, for example, have been particularly hard hit. In addition, as we discussed in Chapter Four, the Afro-Cuban population has been disproportionately affected by such reforms as the dollarization of the economy, by the general exclusion of blacks from the expansion of the tourist sector, and by uneven access to Cuba's small private sector, where wages are substantially higher than in the dominant state sector. By contrast, those who are part of the regime, as well as those who have been able to participate in the private sector, have fared much better.

On balance, as Mesa-Lago (2002) reports, the net effect of the cutbacks in the social safety net and the economic collapse has been a dramatic increase in inequality within Cuba. Thus, it is particularly ironic that Cuba's social safety net, generally viewed as one of the regime's real accomplishments, is in shambles when it is most needed.

The collapse of Cuba's social services, just as much as the collapse of the Soviet Union and the failure of communism more generally, symbolizes the failure of the Castro regime and of the Revolution. As Fernández (see Appendix B) points out, this experience has contributed to the population's general disillusionment with the regime and the Revolution.

Given this experience and the fact that many of the population groups most adversely affected during the Special Period are quite skeptical about economic liberalization, it seems likely that Castro's successors will attempt to repair the social service system to gain political legitimacy as well as popular support for their future policies. However, their efforts to do so will be hampered by Cuba's emerging demographic structure.

CHAPTER FIVE

Cuba's Changing Demographic Structure[1]

When discussing future population prospects, demographers typically sort the nations of the world according to where their population structures fall within the demographic transition. The *demographic transition* describes the historical pattern of population growth in terms of an ordered sequence of changes in birth and death rates and how the interaction of those rates shapes a country's growth prospects. The transition begins with birth and death rates in rough equilibrium at high levels. Sustained population growth begins when death rates begin to fall, slows after birth rates eventually begin to decline, and effectively stops when birth and death rates reach a new equilibrium at low levels. A country's age structure plays a critical role in this transition. Declining death rates and continued high fertility produce an age structure dominated by youth. Such a youthful age structure helps perpetuate population growth even after fertility rates begin to decline. Eventually, however, low fertility and mortality not only slow population growth to a trickle, they also produce an aging-population age structure.

When assessed in these terms, Cuba has clearly completed the demographic transition. Its population has been growing at less than 1 percent per year since 1980 and is projected to grow at an annual rate of less than 0.2 percent between now and 2025 (McCarthy, 2004, Appendix C). Moreover, its birth and death rates resemble

---

[1] A more complete discussion of the demographic transition can be found in (McCarthy, 2004, Appendix C).

much more closely those of the developed world than those of the less-developed world or Cuba's neighbors in Latin America and the Caribbean. Indeed, although Cuba appears to have started the demographic transition somewhat later than the developed world has, its fertility and mortality rates, as well as its age structure, are quite similar to the slow-growing and aging populations of developed countries.

This parallel is important because, by and large, a country's population structure is inversely related to its level of development— i.e., countries characterized by rapid growth and a young age structure are also characterized by low per-capita incomes and less development, whereas those with an aging population and slow population growth generally have higher incomes and more advanced levels of economic development. Cuba clearly does not fit this pattern.

Virtually all demographic phenomena (births, deaths, marriage, and migration), many economic behaviors (entering and retiring from the labor force), and major consumption decisions typically occur within certain age ranges. From a societal point of view, three age groups are particularly noteworthy: the young population (both preschoolers and those who are still in school); the working population; and those who have retired from the labor force. Although the services they use differ, both the young and retired populations are intensive service users. By contrast, the costs of providing these services are largely borne by the working-age population. Thus, the relative sizes of these different age groups will directly affect both the demand for services and the ability to provide those services.

This fact does not bode well for Cuba's future, since the most rapidly growing segment of its population during the next two decades will be its older population (65 and over). Its workforce will be growing progressively older while its younger population will be decreasing. In sum, the demand for services (at least among its older population) will be increasing, and its working population will be growing older and eventually decreasing.

Thus, like all countries in similar demographic circumstances, Cuba will face three critical issues as it attempts to cope with an aging population:

- First, how will it support its aging population?
- Second, how will it allocate its scarce resources among its various social programs?
- Third, how will it provide the labor force to pay for what seems certain to be an increase in social expenditures?

Cuba's ability to restore its social service sector will hinge on how the Cuban government responds to these questions. However, unlike most countries facing these issues, Cuba's level of development, its ideological orientation, and its institutional history will make crafting policy solutions to these problems particularly difficult—and, quite likely, politically divisive.

Pensions

Because Cuba completed the demographic transition about two decades later than most of the developed countries, the effects of aging on its population are only just beginning to be felt. Nonetheless, the pressures of supporting its retired population are already placing stress on Cuba's resources, and that stress has been growing during the current economic crisis. Pérez (1998), for example, estimates that the cost of Cuba's pension system has increased from 5.3 percent of the country's GDP in 1989 to 6.7 percent in 1997. Pérez-López (2002), on the other hand, estimates the cost at 13 percent of the GNP.[2]

Whatever the precise figure, the cost is clearly large and growing. And, as Pérez has pointed out, Cuba's pension system, already facing a large unfunded liability, has seen the size of that deficit grow from 417 million pesos in 1989 to 712 million pesos in 1997. Given cur-

---

[2] The concepts of GDP and GNP are related measures of the gross output of an economy—i.e., the value of goods and services produced by an economy. They differ in how they allocate the value of the inputs used in production. GDP allocates the value of inputs to the location of the owners of the input. GNP allocates the value of the inputs to the nationality of those owners. GDP is increasingly the more preferred measure. Typically, GNP is higher than GDP.

rent per-capita expenditure levels and the expected increases in Cuba's retirement-age population, we estimate that the government's total outlays for pensions will increase at least 50 percent over the next two decades.

Cuba's current economic crisis and the aging of its population are, however, not the only causes of the stress facing Cuba's pension system. Cubans, for example, qualify for pensions from the state at younger ages (55 for women; 60 for men) than in most other countries; thus, the pressures of supporting an aging population will be felt earlier in Cuba than elsewhere. In addition, as retirees live longer (the most-rapidly growing age group in Cuba is over 80), pensioners will be receiving payments for longer periods. The burden of paying these pensions, moreover, falls overwhelmingly on the public sector, both because the state sector dominates total employment and because the state does not require its workers to contribute to their retirement. Finally, Cuba operates its public pension system on a "pay-as-you-go" basis, so that the funds needed to pay annual pension costs are supplied by current revenues rather than by reserves set aside for that purpose.

These features of Cuba's current pension system simply compound the problems posed by the aging of its population. Indeed, it seems almost certain that future Cuban governments will be required to revamp the current system to keep it from collapsing, rather than restore it to its status prior to the onset of the current Special Period. However, many of the policy options that other countries are considering in response to similar demographic pressures are likely to have undesirable ripple effects of their own.

Three sets of such changes have been considered elsewhere. One involves reducing the annual payout by reducing the pool of eligibles, either by raising the retirement age or introducing a means test for eligibility or by lowering the average annual pension amount. However, given the declining real value of Cuba's current pensions and the cutbacks in food and housing subsidies, such policies would likely compound the population's disillusionment with the regime and the support it will require for broader economic reforms.[3]

A second type of reform would involve increasing the revenues paid into the system by requiring employees to contribute to their own retirement, as many other countries do. Once again the depressed state of the current Cuban economy and the declining real value of wages (especially in the public sector) would likely generate political opposition to such a policy. This opposition might be particularly pronounced among younger workers, who would likely bear the primary burden of such a policy, and might also engender conflicts among age groups.

A third type of reform might involve shifting private-sector employers' and employees' role in financing pensions. Despite the recent liberalization of Cuba's economy and the emergence of a small but significant private sector (in which wages are higher and employment has grown much more rapidly than in the public sector), any policy that relied on the private sector as a major solution to Cuba's pension problems would require reversal in Cuba's economic policy away from a centrally planned economy toward a private-enterprise model. For ideological and historical reasons, such a reversal appears to be anathema for the Castro regime and of uncertain appeal to its successors. It would also impose a heavy burden on the fledgling private sector.

The Allocation of Social Service Resources

Although the problems that an aging society poses for Cuba may be the most obvious, the demographic changes Cuba is currently experiencing and that will intensify in the near future, will also force the Cuban leadership to decide how to allocate its social spending to sat-

---

[3] Mesa-Lago (2002) reports that the average real value of average pensions has declined by over 40 percent during the Special Period and that the base public pension now amounts to $4 per month, despite cutbacks in subsidies for food and housing and the fact that many commodities are now available only in dollar stores, where prices are not subsidized.

isfy competing social service demands. This allocation problem is in part a consequence of the collapse of the Cuban economy since the withdrawal of Soviet aid. But it also has a growing demographic dimension.

As we noted above, Cuba's changing demographic structure has highlighted the different interest of the two groups of intensive service users (the young and the old) vis-à-vis those of the working-age population, who bear the primary costs of providing those services. Thus, Cuba's changing demographic profile raises two central questions for Cuba's policymakers: First, how much of the GDP should be spent on social services? Second, how should those funds be allocated between services for the young and services for the old?

The first of these questions entails deciding how much of Cuba's economic output should be spent on current consumption as opposed to investment for future economic growth. Over the long term, higher levels of economic investment will yield higher incomes and, thus, more resources for future consumption. However, unlike most other societies with an aging population, Cuba's low-levels of income and economic development make decisions to cut back current consumption in the interest of future growth particularly painful. It is interesting to note, for example, that the Castro regime initially attempted to maintain social-spending levels subsequent to the withdrawal of Soviet aid, but it was eventually forced to cut back social spending for macro-economic reasons (Hernandez-Cata, 2000). Moreover, several observers of Cuba's current economic predicament suggest that further cuts in consumption may be impossible (Erikson and Wolf, 2002; Mesa-Lago, 2003a).

However the government decides to allocate its scarce resources, that choice is likely to produce adverse political fallout. Further cuts in current consumption will likely alienate those who depend most on government services. Maintaining social services, on the other hand, will increase the burden on Cuba's workers, who have already absorbed cutbacks in real wages. Moreover, these effects may be particularly pronounced on Cuba's youth. And, as we have already noted, these youth are profoundly disenchanted with the Revolution. Indeed, the prospect of continued economic hardships may well increase incentives either to emigrate, if possible, or to compound the corruption and making-do approach that have clearly grown during the Special Period.

The second choice, how to allocate social spending between the young and the old, might, at first glance, appear more straightforward, since a decline in the school-aged population would, all else being equal, result in a decline in total expenditures for the young, especially for education. Indeed, Donate-Armada (2001) projects that a decline in the number of youth will reduce educational expenditures by 20 percent over the next 20 years, at current per-capita expenditure levels. However, such a reduction would be substantially smaller than the increase in expenditures for pensions and health care. We estimate that pension expenditures will increase by at least 50 percent and, because patterns of health-care usage vary by age, health care expenditures could increase by close to 25 percent with the aging of Cuba's population.[4]

However, given the importance of an educated population to Cuba's future economic growth, it is unclear that a cutback in educational expenditures would make economic sense. Specifically, given an essentially stable number of workers (indeed, Cuba's labor force will start to decline within the next two decades), Cuba's future economic growth is much more likely to depend upon the quality of its labor force than upon the quantity. To improve that quality, Cuba will need to invest more in education rather than less.

Indeed, as Pérez-López (2004, Appendix D) discusses, one of the major problems facing the economy currently is the low correlation between educational achievement and productivity. This situation reflects the priorities embedded in the regime's current educational policies, which emphasize expanding access to previously excluded groups at the primary and secondary levels rather than pro-

---

[4] Mesa-Lago (2002) reports that Cuba's combined expenditures for health care and pensions are roughly twice its expenditures for education. Our estimate of the effect of aging on health-care expenditures is based on the age-related patterns of health-care usage and expenditures in the United States. Although health-care expenditures in the United States are undoubtedly much higher than in Cuba, our estimates depend upon the differential patterns of expenditures by age, not their levels (Center for Cost and Financing Studies, 1996).

moting achievement and the development of needed economic skills at the university level.[5] Moreover, access to higher education in Cuba has been determined more on the basis of ideological conformity, family connections, and allegiance to the regime than on performance per se (Gasperini, 2000; Mesa-Lago, 2002).

In sum, although Cuba's changing demographic structure would appear to indicate that resources should be shifted from the youth to the aged, such a policy would appear to be short-sighted: Since the country's future economic growth will hinge more on the quality than on the quantity of its labor force, emphasis would be better placed on improving labor's productivity. This emphasis, in turn, will require not only an increased investment in educating and training current and future workers but also a major reorganization of Cuba's educational system.

Securing a Future Labor Force

As we have suggested above, the key to restoring Cuba's social service programs in the future will be how fast its economy and worker productivity grow. However, the same demographic forces that will increase the demand for services could work against more rapid economic growth. Specifically, the aging of Cuba's population will reduce the size of the future cohorts that will be entering the labor force. For example, the ratio of new labor-force entrants (the population 15 to 19 years old) to those exiting the labor force (the population 60 to 64 years old) is currently 1.25; between 2001 and 2005, this figure will increase slightly to 1.38 between 2006 and 2010 and then drop to 1.12 between 2011 and 2015 and to 0.97 between 2016 and 2020. In other words, within the next 15 to 20 years, Cuba's

---

[5] As Donate-Armada (2001) indicates, expenditures per pupil have been considerably higher at the primary- and secondary-educational level than at the higher-education level. This may well account for the fact that the major economic effect of Cuba's educational policies has been the growth in agricultural productivity associated with eliminating illiteracy among Cuba's agricultural workers (Madrid-Aris, 2000).

working-age population will start to contract (as well as to grow older).

Although population growth is not a necessary condition for economic growth, a shrinking labor force can pose serious challenges for an economy—particularly a developing economy characterized by low labor productivity and a shortage of investment capital, such as Cuba's. In most developing countries, population growth typically produces a rapidly growing workforce that correspondingly expands the base of earnings from which to fund social services. Labor is typically the only one of the three factors of production (natural resources, capital, and labor) that many developing countries have in abundance, and such countries often rely on that ample labor supply (typically at low wage levels) to attract investment capital.

Cuba, however, is in a very different situation. It not only has a shortage of investment capital and limited natural resources, it also is facing a shrinking labor pool. Correspondingly, it will need to consider various options for meeting its future labor needs by expanding the size of its workforce. It might, for example, raise the retirement age—a policy that would both increase the labor supply and postpone the onset of pensions. A second option would be to increase the labor-force participation among prime-age workers. Finally, it might attempt to increase the immigration of foreign workers, as other countries with an aging population have done.

Each of these options is likely to require the Cuban government to provide greater incentives for workers. Currently, wages in the state sector are set according to a national pay schedule, not by workers' contribution to productivity. Thus, workers have little incentive to increase their work efforts. Moreover, the Castro regime, as Pérez-López and others have noted, has placed a higher priority on maintaining full employment than on promoting economic efficiency. The result has been substantial underemployment of the Cuban workforce. The regime's resistance to expanding the private sector, instead of subsidizing unproductive state enterprises, has also contributed to this problem. Hernández-Cata, for example, estimates that all of the new jobs created during the Special Period have been in the private sector. Yet, the Castro regime, after initially legalizing self-employment, subsequently imposed a series of restrictions that have made it increasingly difficult to start a private business and, for private firms, to hire nonfamily employees.[6] Indeed, despite the fact that many professionals have been moving from high-skilled but low-paying jobs in the state sector to lower-skilled but higher-paying jobs in the tourism and private sectors, the government prohibits professionals holding university degrees from starting a self-employed business in the occupations in which they have been trained (Pérez-López, 2002).

In large part, the underlying rationale for the Castro regime's unwillingness to relax these policies has been its recognition that to do so would increase the degree of inequality in earnings and income within the Cuban population. Nonetheless, as Mesa-Lago has reported, earnings and income inequality in Cuba have increased sharply during the Special Period.[7] Indeed, even Fidel Castro seemed to have recognized the tensions between economic equality and efficiency in a recent speech when he noted:

> One of the things for which the Revolution can be reproached is that it has brought too much equality; it managed to establish egalitarianism and this had to be rectified because it wasn't working and it *works even less in a situation of poverty. The more poverty there is, the less egalitarianism works.* . . . These changes (the reforms introduced) were inevitable and we have to make some more which foster individualism, selfishness, and make the value of money more important. [emphasis added]. Quoted in Mesa-Lago (2001).

How a post-Castro regime will respond to these demographic pressures is uncertain. As Mesa-Lago (2001) has indicated, there has been considerable debate within Cuba about the need for further re-

---

[6] These restrictive policies include extensive licensing, increased fees and taxes, and limiting hiring to family members (Hernández-Cata, 2000).

[7] Although the Cuban government reports no data on income distributions, Mesa-Lago (2002) estimates that the maximum wage differential among Cuban workers has grown from 4.5 to 1 in 1989 to 829 to 1 in 1995. He also provides a range of other forms of increasing inequality.

forms within the socialist context. We might expect that debate to become broader and more open when Castro is no longer on the scene. But as other countries in similar demographic circumstances have discovered, the central issue in the debate about equity versus economic efficiency revolves around the question of who wins and who loses as a result of these decisions.

Indeed, each of the three issues we have discussed above essentially revolves around the priority society attaches to the interests of different groups: workers versus retirees, the young versus the old, urban versus rural residents, and Afro-Cubans versus whites. Castro has tried, with considerable success up until the Special Period, to sublimate these potential tensions through policies designed to equalize the distribution of resources among Cuba's residents. It is unclear whether Castro or his successors will continue to be able to do so.

However, as the Special Period and Castro's own admission cited above have made abundantly clear, this policy is no longer working and Cuba's emerging demographic structure will make past policies even less tenable. Over the long term, Cuba's ability to restore its social service programs would seem to depend upon its willingness to reinvigorate its economy. But it may prove ironic that the Revolution's traditional commitment to promoting equity at the expense of economic efficiency may make it even more difficult for any successor regime to institute the economic reforms that would seem to be necessary to support those very programs.

CHAPTER SIX

The Institutional Legacy of a Centralized Economy

As we have just discussed, perhaps the key structural imperative for both the current and future Cuban governments is to develop policies that will generate rapid economic growth. However, just as Cuba must overcome the obstacles to achieving that objective, which arise from its changing demographic structure, so too the government will have to overcome two major economic challenges. First, it will need to overcome the institutional legacy of economic practices and institutions that have developed during the four-and-a-half decades during which the Castro government pursued a series of policies based on the Soviet model of a socialist, centrally planned economy (CPE). Second, it will need to revamp an industrial structure spawned by Cuba's relations with the Soviet Union that has left it ill-prepared to integrate into an increasingly global economy. As the experience of the former Soviet bloc countries demonstrates, overcoming these challenges is not a straightforward task, and the required transition typically takes longer than reformers envision.

The central features of Cuba's economic model are state ownership of productive resources, concentration of economic decision-making in the hands of central government planners, and a planning model in which the allocation of resources, wages, and most prices is determined by political decisions rather than by the market.

With the exception of the railroads, most of Cuba's productive resources were privately owned prior to the Revolution. As a result of the aggressive nationalization program that Castro pursued in the years following his ascension to power, private ownership was essentially eliminated in Cuba by 1968, with the exception of the agricultural sector—30 percent of which was still in private hands. However, state seizure of agricultural land was aggressively pursued and, by 1988, the state controlled 92 percent of agricultural land as well (Rodríguez, 1990).

Since the onset of the Special Period, the Cuban government has experimented with various forms of privatization—e.g. the breakup of state farms into Basic Units of Cooperative Production (*Unidades Basicas de Produción Cooperativa*), the establishment of joint ventures with foreign investors, privatized state enterprises (*sociedades anonimas*), and small businesses owned by self-employed workers. However, close to 80 percent of total employment remained in the state sector by the turn of the century (Oficina Nacional de Estadísticas [ONE], 2001).

In addition to its program of nationalizing economic resources, the Castro regime also began a program of centralized economic planning shortly after the Revolution. By the mid-1960s, it had become a full-scope command economy (Pérez-López, 2003). In a centrally planned command economy, such as Cuba's, all resource-allocation decisions are made administratively and incorporated in the central plan. The central plan lays out input and output targets for each ministry and geographic division. Prices and wages are also set by fiat, as are targets for foreign trade. In addition to its administrative complexity, this form of planning makes it extremely difficult to respond quickly to changes in economic circumstances; thus, chronic shortages of goods and services typically result. These shortages, in turn, lead to rationing and the emergence of black markets. Both rationing and black markets are characteristic of the Cuban economy.

The problems of central planning are particularly problematic for labor allocation. Cuban central planning is designed to provide full employment, with all workers guaranteed a job. State-owned enterprises are told the number of workers they must hire in order to meet full-employment goals. Once hired, workers are almost impossible to terminate. Workers, in turn, are paid according to a national pay schedule rather than their contribution to output. This system has produced a combination of low wages, a low level of work effort, and generalized job dissatisfaction (Pérez-López, 2003).

The problems that such politically driven economic policies have produced are typified by the government's decision to raise sugar output to 10 million tons in 1970. Resources were diverted from other sectors and reallocated to the sugar campaign. Despite this massive effort, Cuba failed to meet the harvest goal and the disruptions caused to other sectors of the economy were severe.

Given these problems, the Cuban government under Castro has considered a variety of modifications to the CPE model. Perhaps the most notable was the *Sistema de Dirección y Planificación de la Economía* (SDPE), which promoted some decentralization of economic decisionmaking and introduced various forms of profit and cost indicators. Cuba has also experimented with other market-oriented reforms, such as the Free Peasant Markets in the 1980s. However, the Castro regime, most particularly Castro himself, has been reluctant to cede control over key economic decisions (Espinosa and Harding, 2000), and these reforms have subsequently either been abandoned or cut back. These policies, together with the economic crisis of the Special Period, have wrecked havoc with Cuba's central planning system.

After four-and-a-half decades, the Cuban economic model has left a profound and dysfunctional legacy for the economy that will need to be dealt with by Castro's successors if they are to revitalize the economy. The most notable of these legacies are a highly educated but low-productivity labor force, a small and deformed private sector, and rampant corruption. Each of these legacies will now be discussed in turn.

Cuba's Highly Educated but Low-Productivity Labor Force

As we discussed above, Cuba is certain to face problems meeting its labor needs in the future, as the size of its workforce stabilizes and eventually begins to decline. As a result, Cuba's future economic growth will increasingly depend upon the quality and productivity of its workers. And, in light of the high levels of education among its population, Cuba would appear to be well positioned to meet this challenge. Indeed, it is axiomatic in the human capital literature that education enhances worker productivity. However, one of the central paradoxes of Cuba's socialist legacy is that, despite its highly educated workforce, it has abysmally low levels of worker productivity.

Mesa-Lago (2000), for example, concludes that labor productivity growth during the period 1971 to 1985—arguably the period of strongest growth of the Cuban economy—was low and well below planned targets. In fact, he argues that if 1981 data are excluded, average productivity growth during this period was negative, consistent with other information on the underutilization of labor across several sectors of the economy (Pérez-López, 2004, Appendix D).

Madrid-Aris (2000), for example, concludes that the effects of Cuba's aggressive expansion of free education were small and mostly associated with eliminating illiteracy among agricultural workers. Mesa-Lago also notes that productivity declined at an average annual rate of 2.6 percent during the second half of the 1980s instead of achieving a planned annual increase of 3.5 percent. Although Cuba publishes no data on productivity, the weak relationship between productivity and education has probably become even more pronounced during the Special Period, which began in 1990 with the widely reported movement of professionally trained workers into low-skilled jobs in the tourist and private sectors.

Cuba's low productivity levels have no doubt been exacerbated by the declining state of its capital stock, the shortage of investment capital with which to improve that stock, and the lack of raw materials for its industries. However, the Castro government's policies with regard to full employment and wages have also played a major role. Indeed, Cuba's policy of full employment appears to have transformed open unemployment into rampant underemployment:

In 1963, employees of state farms worked an average of 4.5 to 5 hours per day but were paid for 8. Industrial mergers and shutdowns should have generated unemployment, but unneeded workers remained on the enterprise payroll. The tertiary sector became hypertrophied with the expansion of the bureaucracy, social services, the armed forces, and internal security (Mesa-Lago, 2000).

As Pérez-López (2004, Appendix D) notes, "this policy decision had the effect of alleviating the short-term unemployment problem, but it spread the economic costs to the entire population and negatively affected long-term labor productivity and economic growth."

Indeed, the Castro government has continued to pursue this politically driven policy during the Special Period. For example, despite chronic problems within the sugar industry that prompted temporary shutdowns of sugar mills and the eventual closure of more than 45 percent of those mills, the Castro government has kept the displaced workers on the payroll (Pérez-López, 2004, Appendix D). Pérez-López, citing the Economic Commission for Latin America and the Caribbean (2001) report, has noted:

> Cuba's open unemployment rate hovered in the 6 to 7 percent range between 1960 and 1996, while "equivalent unemployment"—an estimate of underemployment—climbed as high as 35.2 percent in 1993; taking open unemployment and underemployment together, over 40 percent of the labor force was not fully employed.

Cuba's policy of setting wages according to a national schedule has compounded this low-productivity problem by divorcing workers' wages from their productivity. As Pérez-López notes, average wages in the state sector have failed to keep up with inflation during that period. Conversely, as Mesa-Lago (2002) notes, wages of workers in the private sector, employees in the tourist sector, and speculators in the black market have risen dramatically. This rise, of course, is one of the major reasons that highly skilled professionals have been leaving their jobs in the state sector and taking low-skilled jobs in the private sector, a situation that has been compounded by the cutback in social services and the fact that many consumer goods are available only in dollar-denominated stores at prices approximating those paid in the world market. Indeed, as Pérez-López notes, the severe shortage of consumer goods and the possibility of being able to obtain such goods in dollar stores means "that time will be taken off from a job that pays in pesos to engage in wheeling and dealing that results in earning dollars."

In combination, these policies have produced poor work habits, lack of on-the-job efforts, and a low-productivity labor force. As the Soviets used to say, "We pretend to work and they pretend to pay us." Overcoming this legacy and motivating the labor force to respond to market incentives is likely to take time, as the experience in Eastern Europe has demonstrated.

A Small and Deformed Private Sector

A variety of analysts have drawn parallels between Cuba and the economic challenges it is facing and the experience of the former communist states of Eastern Europe. Gayoso, (2000), for example, emphasizes the important role small and medium-sized private enterprises (SMEs) have played in facilitating the transition between centrally planned and market economies. As Gayoso notes, SMEs have been a major source of employment growth; they have also promoted efficiency, helped to instill an entrepreneurial spirit, and promoted experience with market mechanisms. The robust response of Cubans to the Castro regime's liberalization of policies with regard to self-employment in 1993 would seem to support Gayoso's points. As both Mesa-Lago (2001) and Hernandez-Cata (2000) make clear, the modest recovery from the trough of economic decline in 1993 appears to be due primarily to growth in employment and productivity in the self-employed sector. Hernandez-Cata, for example, estimates that while employment in the state sector declined by nearly 750,000 between 1990 and 1998, employment in the private sector increased by almost 600,000—mostly on small private farms and in self-employed enterprises. Pérez-López notes that within six months of the legalization of self-employment, 70,000 individuals had registered for self-employment—a total that grew to more than 200,000 by the end of 1995.

However, as Gayoso also notes, the expansion of the SME sector typically requires major changes in the institutions, practices, and behaviors that have developed during the decades of centralized control, and that the more dominant the state sector is, the more difficult changing these practices can be. By this standard, the problems Cuba will face in the transition to the development of a market economy will be substantial.

Even by the standards of Eastern Europe, Cuba's private sector is very small. All of the major industries in Cuba are owned by the state. In 2000, workers in the private sector amounted to only 13.4 percent of employment. Most of these workers were small agricultural operators (ONE, 2000). Indeed, despite the enthusiastic response to the liberalization of self-employment, the Cuban government's subsequent actions to limit this option by increasing taxes and fees and imposing stricter regulations and government oversight had reduced the number of self-employed workers to 150,000 by 2001.[1]

In addition to government policies discouraging private-sector employment, a variety of other institutional and behavioral obstacles have been put in the way of private employment. As Pérez-López (2004, Appendix D) puts it, Cuba's private sector is not only small, it is precarious and deformed. Institutionally, Cuba lacks any wholesale distribution system from which the private sector can obtain raw materials and equipment, forcing workers and entrepreneurs to resort to the black market or other illegal sources of goods and services. As Jatar-Hausman (1999) notes,

> Cuba has no wholesale distributors. The Cuban government has not opened supply markets. Intermediaries are not only illegal, but unwanted. . . . (Private sector workers) either take supplies from their workplace (in other words, steal them) or they buy them in the black market. Where do the products in the black market come from? From other workers who do the same thing. Everyone has to steal in Cuba for survival.

---

[1] A description of these policies can be found in Mesa-Lago (2001). The experience of private restaurants (*paladares*), one of the major types of self-employment, is discussed in Henken (2002).

Moreover, 40-plus years of communism have wiped out the market-oriented skills that are critical to the operation of a market economy. These include such skills as those of managers, accountants, auditors, bankers, and insurers. As Pérez-López puts it, the several generations of Cubans who have grown up under socialism have meager market-oriented skills. Overcoming these institutional and behavioral obstacles will be a difficult task, even if future Cuban governments adopt market-oriented policies. And Castro has so far proved unwilling to aggressively pursue policies to accomplish these changes.

Corruption

As we have just described, one of the major obstacles to the development of a market economy is the extensive reliance that Cubans have developed on the black market and other illegal practices. The institutional counterpart to such behavior at the individual level is the widespread practice of corruption and the lack of institutional safeguards to limit and address corrupt practices. As Pérez-López and others have noted, the widespread reliance on corruption is a familiar feature of centrally directed and socialist economies.

Corrupt practices take several forms in Cuba. The pervasive presence of black markets not only for food and consumer goods, which are ostensibly covered by the official rationing system, but also in virtually all areas of the economy, fuel corruption, because most of the materials sold on the black market are stolen or misappropriated from government property. In addition to direct theft of government materials, corruption in the form of bribes, influence-peddling, and reliance on insider contacts to influence government decisions or gain priority for such services as installing telephones and exchanging homes abounds. Indeed, Cubans have coined the word "*sociolismo*" (a corruption of buddy, "*socio*," and *socialismo*) to refer to the use of government contacts for personal gain.

Corruption is also manifest in the numerous special privileges that members of the regime (the *nomenklatura*, referred to as *pinchos* or *pinchos grandes* in Cuba) enjoy because of their position. As Pérez-López notes, these privileges include exemption from the community rationing to which the general population is subject, access to imported consumer goods and special housing, use of government vehicles, treatment in special hospitals, the ability to travel abroad, and admission to special schools for their children.

Since the onset of the Special Period and the government's selective privatization of state enterprises, a new form of corruption has emerged: High-ranking members of the *nomenklatura* have been made owners or directors of former state enterprises. This practice, referred to as "spontaneous privatization," bestows state assets on individuals loyal to the regime without their investing either financial or human capital in these enterprises. By the early 1990s, more than 60 of these enterprises, referred to as *sociedades anonimas*, had been created, often in those sectors of the economy that generate hard currency and foreign investment (Pérez-López, 2004, Appendix D). As Kaufmann and Siegelbaum (1997) note, this practice "is the very essence of corruption, being the outright theft of public assets by politicians and or enterprise directors associated with the nomenklatura."

Although it is difficult to estimate the economic effects of corruption precisely, corruption has been widely recognized as an important obstacle to economic development and growth (World Bank, 1999). Gray and Kaufman (1998), for example, report that when officials from more than 60 developing countries were surveyed they cited corruption as the major obstacle to economic development. Mauro (1995, 1997) has confirmed the negative association between corruption and economic development empirically.

There are a wide variety of ways in which corruption can impede growth. Bribes extracted by government officials, for example, represent a tax on economic activity, but that tax is appropriated by private individuals (the officials) rather than placed in the public coffers. Moreover, to the extent that these implicit taxes must be compensated for by higher taxes on those who comply with the law rather than bribing officials, then those who play by the rules pay a penalty in the form of higher taxes. Rewarding those who offer bribes for government contracts, the allocation of licenses and positions, etc., will often result in the misallocation of talent and resources and may reduce the quality of goods and services provided, all of which involve economic costs to society. Moreover, to the extent that donor countries become aware of corrupt practices, they may reduce the level of aid they provide. Finally, widespread corruption undermines the legitimacy of the state and can provoke widespread public cynicism about the government and its programs—a phenomenon that appears to be increasingly apparent in Cuba.

Although corruption no doubt existed in Cuba before the Revolution, it has been endemic since then and appears to have increased during the Special Period. The reasons for this phenomenon are suggested by Klitgaard (1988), who identifies corruption as a product of the degree of monopoly exercised by the state over economic resources, the discretion government agencies have in allocating those resources, and the degree of accountability to which the government is subject. Cuba's rating on each of these dimensions promotes high levels of corruption. As we have already noted, the state exercises a monopoly on major enterprises and, with the exception of a small private sector, controls the whole economy, which, of course, magnifies the potential for corruption. Second, the extensive economic planning in which the government sets output targets, allocates inputs, and sets prices requires an enormous bureaucracy and cedes considerable discretion to that bureaucracy. Finally, the overwhelming power of the government and its ruling party limit the public accountability to which the government is subject. In sum, the Cuban governmental arrangement seems particularly well suited toward promoting corruption. Even after Castro is no longer on the scene, this potential for corruption will remain unless the underlying CPE model is changed.

Reducing the central government's role in the economy alone, however, deals only with the opportunities for corruption. It is also important to increase the degree to which government officials are accountable to the public. Cuba's current policies limit governmental accountability is several major ways. First, there are no free elections; instead, the electorate is limited to endorsing a slate of Party candidates. Second, key governmental decisions are made in secret, by

Fidel and his inner circle. Third, the government controls key institutions, such as the press and the judiciary, which in open societies act to expose governmental actions to public scrutiny and punish government wrongdoers. Finally, as we discussed above, the government has actively suppressed independent civil organizations, despite the Law of Associations, which purportedly guarantees the right of Cuban citizens to associate freely. However, as the recent crackdown by the government once again demonstrates, the Castro regime has repeatedly thwarted the development of the organizations that are key to a robust civil society.

CHAPTER SEVEN

The Need for Industrial Restructuring

In addition to the institutional legacy of a centrally planned economy, Cuba's economy has also been harmed by development policies that have left it ill prepared to compete in the world economy. Unlike countries that have pursued development policies designed to enable them to compete in an increasingly global economy, Cuba's development policies, up until the Special Period, went in an entirely different direction. Rather than develop an industrial structure that would enable Cuba to compete in world markets, it relied, instead, on its special economic relationship with the Soviet Union and the other states of the Council for Mutual Economic Assistance to insulate it from global market forces. The collapses of the Soviet Union and the CMEA have subsequently left Cuba's economy and its industrial structure ill suited to competing effectively in world markets.

Although the Castro regime has adopted policies designed to remedy some of the adjustment problems it faces, it has not fully committed to these policies. In this chapter, we first discuss the nature of Cuba's special economic relationship with the Soviet Union and the effect that relationship has had on Cuba's industrial structure. We then discuss the policies Cuba has adopted in response to its changing circumstances. Finally, we conclude by discussing Cuba's intermediate economic prospects.

The Effects of Soviet Assistance on the Cuban Economy

Prior to the Revolution, Cuba's economic fortunes were closely tied to the sugar industry. As Pérez-López (2004, Appendix E) puts it,

> Sugar was the engine that powered the Cuban economy. Sugar production was the main industrial activity, the main generator of foreign exchange, and the largest single employer in the nation. . . . When the international market price was high, the island experienced a period of economic prosperity referred to as *vacas gordas*; this was invariably followed by prolonged periods of low sugar prices and *vacas flacas*.

By the end of the 1950s, Cuba had begun the process of industrialization and the development of its tourist industry. Most of Cuba's trade, both in sugar and industrial inputs, was focused on the United States, which was also the primary source of investment capital (Economic Commission for Latin America and the Caribbean, 2001).

Cuba's development process after the Revolution became dependent instead on the Soviet Union and the other CMEA states. These ties to the CMEA, which insulated Cuba from the international market, also shaped its industrial development in ways that left it particularly unprepared for integrating into the world economy after the CMEA collapsed. The central feature of the Cuban-CMEA relationship was the exchange of Cuban sugar for CMEA investment, equipment, and technology.

This exchange transformed the Cuban economy in a variety of ways. First, in response to the extremely favorable prices the CMEA states paid for Cuban sugar,[1] the Castro regime, rather than diversifying its industrial base, concentrated its resources on sugar production and sugar by-products. Indeed, for sugar production during the 1980s, Cuba devoted a third of its investment, about half of its total

---

[1] At the end of the 1980s, the CMEA states were paying the equivalent of $690 per metric ton for raw sugar at the same time as the price in international markets was between $133 and $282 per metric ton (Economic Commission for Latin America and the Caribbean, 2001).

cultivated land, nearly half of its stock of agricultural tractors, about three-quarters of its railway system, and close to a third of its labor (Pérez-López, 2004, Appendix E).

Second, after a disastrous effort to reach a record harvest in 1970 by mobilizing a vast array of temporary labor, Cuba's sugar industry, as well as its agricultural sector more generally, became heavily dependent upon imported inputs (fertilizers, machinery, and energy). As a result of this concentration of resources in sugarcane production and related industries, Cuba has failed to diversify its agricultural production enough to reach self-sufficiency in agriculture. In turn, it has had to rely on imports to fill about half of the country's nutritional requirements—a proportion that appears to have risen during the Special Period (Economic Commission for Latin America and the Caribbean, 2001).

Third, investment in Cuba's incipient industrial sector was concentrated on domestic production of inputs into the sugar industry, including fertilizers, pesticides, animal feeds, packaging, and machinery, and into the development of industries based on sugarcane by-products. Thus, Cuba failed to reach the diversification of its industrial base needed to meet domestic needs, much less to begin to develop foreign markets in higher-value industrial goods.

Fourth, Cuba imported its machinery from the CMEA. This practice not only produced a problem of compatibility with existing equipment that had been imported from the West, it also resulted in a reliance on technologically inferior equipment that further limited efficiency and productivity. Moreover, this equipment was designed for conditions in the Soviet Union, which were often vastly different than conditions in Cuba: Soviet equipment was designed for very large and highly specialized plants and was energy intensive (Economic Commission for Latin America and the Caribbean, 2001). This practice promoted extensive vertical integration of production and thus impeded the development of the industrial linkages necessary for the development of smaller-scale domestic suppliers.

The United Nation's Economic Commission on Latin America and the Caribbean (2001) has summarized the consequences of

Cuba's interdependence with the CMEA for Cuba's economic structure, as follows:

- Considerable dependence on external sources of raw materials and components for products earmarked for the domestic market and imports of inputs tied to exports.
- Industrial plants and equipment that were largely characterized by technological obsolescence, oversized facilities, and difficulties in acquiring spare parts and other hurdles to their normal use.
- An industrial structure with few domestic linkages, dominated by large-scale companies that displayed an excessive degree of vertical integration, thus leaving little room in which smaller enterprises could function.
- Diminished plant efficiencies and flexibilities as a result of technological reasons, excessive machinery, a lack of inputs, and other restrictions.
- Low development of complementary services, which existing plants were largely left to provide—a practice that led to additional inefficiencies.
- Distortions in the characteristics and breakdown of management-level personnel and an excessive number of professional and technically skilled workers, combined with a shortage of employees with experience in marketing, finances, and business administration and management.
- Highly differentiated priorities in allocating foreign currencies and energy inputs, which arose from the stranglehold stemming from the breakdown in economic relations with the CMEA countries.
- Industrial specialization that was a vestige of relations with the CMEA countries, which had often been detrimental to Cuban interests.

Nonetheless, the favorable prices the CMEA was willing to pay for Cuban sugar, the generous credits and grants the CMEA provided, and the Cuban government's political affiliation with the Soviets resulted in close to 80 percent of Cuba's trade being concentrated with CMEA. The net result, however, was a distorted and inefficient industrial structure that not only triggered the economic crisis of the Special Period when the CMEA collapsed but also left the Cuban economy ill prepared to reintegrate itself into the world economy.

Cuba's Development Policies During the Special Period

Given Cuba's dependence on the CMEA and the Soviets in particular, it is not surprising that the collapse of the Soviet Union and the CMEA trade bloc triggered a profound crisis for the Cuban economy. Overnight, Cuba lost the dominant market for its exports,[2] the major supplier of the many inputs for its agriculture and industries, and the principal source of its investment capital. Correspondingly, the economic fallout from the loss of Cuba's special relationship with the CMEA bloc was felt not only in its exports of sugar—its source of foreign earnings—but throughout the Cuban economy. Production collapsed, imports and exports plunged, and Cuba's foreign debt rose sharply.[3]

After an initial attempt at "readjustment by brute force" (Hernández-Cata, 2000), the Cuban regime was forced to adopt a development strategy that focused on obtaining much-needed hard currency by promoting its exports at the same time that it reduced its expenditures for imports through a policy of import substitution—a course change that it was ill prepared to make due to the legacy of overwhelming dependence on trade with the CMEA. Production of

---

[2] Although Cuba continues to trade with Russia, the share of its exports to the former Soviet Union had declined from 65 percent in 1989 to 7 percent in 2000. More important, the former Soviet Union and the other former members of the CMEA are no longer willing to pay exorbitant prices for Cuban sugar, to provide very generous development grants, or to supply large quantities of oil at reduced prices, which Cuba, after meeting its domestic needs, then sold abroad at market prices.

[3] Numerous sources provide details of the economic consequences of this crisis. See, for example, Mesa-Lago (2001), Hernández-Cata (2000), and Economic Commission for Latin America and the Caribbean (2001).

its principal export, sugar, had become inefficient and too dependent upon on imported inputs, with the result that its productive capacity far exceeded its ability to find export markets.[4] As a result, Cuba was forced to cut back its sugar production dramatically (from an annual average of about 8 million tons in 1989 to less than 4 million tons in 2000). This cutback was initially accomplished by temporarily shutting mills; more recently, about one-third of Cuba's mills have been closed permanently (Pérez-López, 2004, Appendix E).

However, this simple downsizing of the sugar industry, in which the worst-performing mills were closed and 60 percent of the lowest-yielding plantations were idled, has not resolved the problems with the industry. Hence, the 2003 harvest plummeted to around 2 million metric tons, almost half the 3.6 million metric tons harvested in 2002, and well below even the industry's own reduced-production goal. Indeed, the 2003 harvest is Cuba's poorest harvest in 70 years. Although on a smaller scale, similar problems of inefficiency and overdependence on imported inputs and lack of the hard currency to purchase those inputs exist throughout Cuba's industrial and agricultural sectors. As a result, production levels in almost all industries have fallen—often dramatically—during the Special Period.

Although sugar remains Cuba's major export, the Cuban government appears to have focused its development efforts on a limited set of products that appear to offer the best prospects for securing hard currency in the international market. Principal among these has been the Cuban government's efforts to develop its tourist industry and expand its nickel and tobacco exports. These efforts have met with some considerable success. In the tourist industry, for example, the number of foreign tourists visiting the island climbed sixfold between 1989 and 2000, accounting for 40 percent of Cuba's hard-currency earnings by 2001, thereby overtaking sugar, rum, tobacco,

---

[4] Cuba, unlike most sugar producers, consumes only a small fraction of its annual total production domestically (roughly 650,000 to 800,000 tons out of a total production from 1970 to 1989 of roughly 7 to 8 million tons. However, the total production costs of Cuban sugar are about 30 percent higher than the world-market price and approximately twice as high as the world's lowest-price producers (Pérez-López, 2004, Appendix E).

and even foreign remittances. By mid-2003, one million tourists had already visited the island, and the goal of two million for the year seemed to be on track, even though industry analysts note that service is shoddy and some foreigners complain of being accosted by peddlers and beggars (Williams, 2003, p. A-3). A favorable world price for nickel and increased output has also made this industry a key export sector for the Cuban economy. World demand for Cuban tobacco has remained strong until recently.[5]

Cuba's new development focus on exporting to international markets and reducing its need for imported goods, in combination with the dollarization of its economy, its policy of encouraging dollar remittances from Cubans in the United States, and limited domestic liberalization, appears to have enabled Cuba to recover somewhat from the massive economic decline during the first three years of the Special Period. Between 1994 and 2000, for example, Cuba's recovery averaged 3.8 percent per annum, its GDP per capita increased by one-quarter, and its exports by more than 50 percent. Still, for the entire 1990–2000 period, the growth rate was –1.2 percent, and Cuba's per-capita GDP remained 25 percent below its level before the Special Period began (Mesa-Lago, 2001). Moreover, Mesa-Lago (2003b) suggests that, after growth rates exceeding 5 percent in 1999 and 2000, the rate of economic growth has slowed once again. Indeed, Cuba's own Ministry of Economy and Planning reported that the GDP expanded by only 1.1 percent in 2002, while forecasting a modest 1.5-percent gain for 2003 (*Cuba News*, February 2003, p. 5).

The Cuban government, at least under Castro's leadership, appears unwilling to fully commit to integration into the world economy—particularly when these efforts appear to challenge its tight political control over its citizens or its underlying Marxist ideology. The regime's unwillingness to let Cuba's economic needs take precedence or interfere with the regime's political dominance is perhaps most apparent in its dealing with the countries of the European Union, the

---

[5] Domestic production of oil has also been a major focus of Cuba's input-substitution policies, and it too has been something of a success (Mesa-Lago, 2001).

principal source of foreign investment in Cuba and its major trading partners.

Despite the willingness of the EU to pursue a policy of engaging Cuba by promoting trade and investment (in contrast to the policies of the United States), Cuba has repeatedly posed institutional obstacles to European investors. Moreover, Cuba has responded to pressures from the EU and its individual countries to relax its human-rights policy by refusing to accept aid with any political conditions. Most recently, Fidel himself has personally criticized Spanish president Jóse María Aznar and derided the EU itself for its criticism and reduction of humanitarian aid in response to Castro's recent crackdown on dissidents in Cuba.

Cuba's Intermediate-Term Economic Prospects

The Cuban government faces a formidable array of obstacles to its efforts to revive its economy. Forty-plus years of Communist central planning have left a legacy of institutional practices that will make increasing domestic productivity difficult. The priority given to equality over efficiency, for example, has promoted low worker productivity and substantial underemployment. Corruption abounds in Cuba and has encouraged a "scratch my back and I'll scratch yours" mentality, which has promoted widespread theft of government property and supported black-market operations in virtually all phases of the economy. The government's ownership of the vast majority of economic resources together with its central planning have discouraged and sometimes outlawed private enterprises and market institutions. This situation has deprived Cuba of the skills that might promote entrepreneurship and the emergence of the small and medium-sized enterprises that have proved to be so important to the transition to market economies in the formerly socialist economies of Eastern Europe. These obstacles to promoting Cuba's domestic economy will be compounded by Cuba's changing demographic structure—in particular, the increasing fraction of the population that will be in retirement and an active labor force that will be both aging and, eventually, shrinking in numbers.

Similarly, Cuba's efforts to generate the foreign earnings so desperately needed to modernize its infrastructure, purchase vital imports, and provide a safety net for its citizens will be hampered by an imbalanced and inefficient industrial structure, much of which was designed to support what is now an uncompetitive and high-cost sugar industry. Moreover, much of Cuba's industrial and agricultural sectors was developed according to a CMEA model that relied on intensive energy use, heavy vertical integration, and intensive use of imported inputs, a model that is ill suited to Cuban economic conditions. Restructuring these sectors will require both human and financial capital, which is currently in very short supply.

Overcoming these obstacles will be particularly difficult, requiring institutional and attitudinal changes, as well as structural changes. To counter the economy's current overreliance on vertically integrated production and its excessive need for imported inputs, for example, Cuba will need to develop integrated supply chains that promote the development of small and medium-sized enterprises. However, entrepreneurs will be reluctant to invest in such enterprises without protection of their property rights, predictable and enforceable contract laws, and some assurances that the regime will not change the rules of the game in midstream. Similarly, capital investment, which Cuba's economy desperately needs and which is most likely to be supplied by foreign investors, will be difficult to attract without enforceable contracts, access to neutral adjudication of disputes, and a degree of predictability that has heretofore been lacking.

However, the need for institutional change is not limited to the business sphere. As we have already discussed, corruption is a major problem in Cuba, and it imposes a tax not only on the economy but on society as well. Combating corruption requires institutions that promote accountability and transparency, such as a free press, impartial and incorruptible legal judicial systems, and a civil society that not only expects but also demands such institutions. Creating such institutions will be difficult in a society in which both the current and successor communist regimes have a stake in maintaining their control, and in which the prerogatives of their position and the population itself is "desocialized." Moreover, as Pérez-López notes (see Appendix D), until such institutions have firmly taken hold, corruption often seems to increase in the transition from centrally planned to market economies, because corruption becomes transformed from "one-stop shopping" to feathering several different nests.

Finally, opening up the Cuban economy to market forces (both internally and externally) will require the Cuban workforce to develop new skills and a new attitude toward work. After four-plus decades of Communist rule, Cuban workers lack both managerial and entrepreneurial skills, as well as many of the more technical skills, such as accounting and marketing, required in a market economy. Perhaps just as important, their work habits have lowered their productivity and have discouraged them from displaying initiative and responding to market incentives.

As a result, Cuba's efforts to secure much-needed hard currency will depend, for the foreseeable future, on the export of primary commodities (nickel, sugar, tobacco) and services (tourism). Yet, each of these industries suffers from many of the same problems that trouble Cuba's economy as a whole: Specifically, they are inefficient, overly dependent upon imported inputs, and in need of substantial capital investment. Moreover, Cuba's reliance on primary commodities makes its exports especially sensitive to commodity market-price fluctuations and external events, such as the aftermath of 9/11, which caused a dramatic drop-off in tourism and the remittances from exiles abroad, over which it has no control.

However, the most significant obstacle to economic recovery in Cuba may well be its government, particularly Castro himself. Although Cuba has embarked on economic reform and liberalization (by necessity rather than by choice), it has been unwilling to sustain and further these reforms when they appear to threaten the *líder máximo*'s ideology or the government's complete political dominance.

CHAPTER EIGHT

Conclusion

Both Fidel Castro and the Revolution he embodies face an uncertain future. Time and age will eventually remove Fidel, who turned 77 in August 2003, from the scene in a way that his enemies could not. His Revolution, on the other hand, faces more immediate and tangible problems. Three of the four pillars on which Cuba's Revolutionary society was built—Soviet economic support, the Revolution's social compact, and the totalitarian state—have already disappeared or have been severely eroded. When the great *caudillo*, the fourth pillar, departs the scene, only the weakened post-totalitarian state's security apparatus, which has been used to control the populace, will be left.

In the meantime, Cuba faces a host of economic, social, and structural problems, which the current regime appears unable or unwilling to solve. As a result, it seems increasingly likely that Castro's successors will be forced to confront these problems. However, their ability to do so is uncertain and will, in any case, require them to operate under very different conditions, balancing the need for economic and social reforms against the regime's compulsion to maintain complete dominance over Cuba's political and economic future.

The Crisis That Won't Go Away

For the first 30-plus years of its existence, the Castro regime demonstrated a remarkable ability to withstand a variety of internal and external challenges. That resilience was in large part due to the combination of the four pillars of support that we described above. When those pillars began to fall with the withdrawal of Soviet support, the consequent "Special Period in a Time of Peace" placed added pressure on the remaining pillars. In particular, the economic strain required to maintain the elaborate social service support structure that the regime had built began to crumble within a few years of the onset of the Special Period. The combination of severe economic contraction and the collapse of the social support system, in turn, undid the social compact and placed serious strains on the general population's allegiance to the regime. Such strains resulted not so much in overt opposition as in a growing disillusionment with the Revolution, and even with the great *caudillo* himself.

In the meantime, the economy's contraction helped transform what had been a totalitarian state into a post-totalitarian state, under which the regime was less able to fully penetrate, control, and mobilize society as it had in the past. Faced with growing political dissent, the regime has been forced to rely increasingly on its extensive security apparatus to suppress dissatisfaction, repress the opposition, and check the emergence of a nascent civil society.

Meanwhile, Cuba's youth, once the hope of the regime, have become increasingly alienated and desocialized, while Afro-Cubans who had earlier benefited from the Revolution have now suffered the most from the economy's contractions and the government's economic policies.

In the face of an unprecedented economic crisis, the regime attempted to check the economic decline and spark recovery by instituting a series of economic reforms, including legalizing the circulation of dollars, allowing self-employment (although on a limited basis), encouraging foreign investors through joint ventures designed to earn hard currency, and promoting the tourist industry. These reforms momentarily checked Cuba's economic slide, although they fell far short of returning output to its level prior to the onset of the Special Period. In the meantime, they generated increasing income inequality. Those who had access to the "new" dollar economy experienced a pronounced improvement in their standard of living, whereas the majority of the population, whose incomes remained tied to the "old" peso economy, saw their standard of living continue to slide.

These reforms also compounded the political problems facing the regime in several ways. First, Afro-Cubans were disproportionately hurt by the reforms, because they had fewer family members abroad sending them dollar remittances; were concentrated in the eastern regions of Cuba, where foreign joint ventures were less present; and were systematically excluded, for racial reasons, from employment in the tourist industry. Indeed, the Special Period rekindled the kind of racial discrimination, especially against blacks, that had long been outlawed, thus re-opening cleavages within the population along racial lines. Second, to make ends meet, the population increasingly resorted to a variety of illegal activities (e.g., participating in the black market, pilfering state resources, engaging in prostitution, and absenting themselves from state employment to earn dollars in the new economy) that furthered disillusionment with the regime, and corrupted society. Third, despite the regime's identification with nationalism, Cubans were generally excluded from dollar stores and tourist areas, making them second-class citizens in their own country. Finally, the need for reform itself became an issue of contention even within the elite, as different factions argued for expanding the reforms, halting further liberalization, and returning to the status quo ante.

After only a few years of liberalization, the hard-liners within the regime won out. This is apparent not only in the reversal of many of the reforms introduced in the mid-1990s but also in the March 18, 2003, crackdown of dissidents and Castro's more recent verbal attacks on the European Union for its criticism of that crackdown, as well as of Cuba's human-rights policies more generally.

As in the past, therefore, the regime remains unwilling to allow economic objectives to interfere with its ideological predispositions and power imperatives. Reversing economic course at this point would be a tacit admission by Castro that his past policies had been wrong in terms of both economics and the course of history—hence, his declaration in 2002 that Cuban socialism was "irreversible." But, just as important, Castro's stance reflects the political need to block economic reforms that widen income inequalities and that could lead to the rise of a new middle class. Indeed, as we have suggested above, the recent crackdown on dissidents was no doubt motivated in part by Castro's desire to remove any remnants of civil society and a nascent opposition in order to facilitate the inevitable transition to his successors.

However, with the near collapse of Cuba's economy and its elaborate social service system, the government is very unlikely to be able to reverse the increasing dissatisfaction of the people and their disillusionment with both the Revolution and the regime. Instead, as has occurred in 2003, it probably will have to continue relying on the state's security apparatus to maintain control over the population.

Thus, the central dilemma facing Cuba is that it needs to introduce decentralization and pluralism in both its society and its economy if it wants its economy to recover, but it is unwilling to surrender either political or economic control even at the cost of a continued slump in the economy. Already the economic recovery that began in the mid-1990s has once again slowed, in large part because of the regime's decision to reverse its policies of economic reform.

Present and Future Structural Challenges

The challenges facing Cuba are not only political, however. The country must also contend with three major structural challenges that are certain to tax any new government: the aging of Cuba's population, the need for institutional change, and the need to revamp the country's economic structure and development policies. These structural challenges will not only compound the island's economic problems, they also will compound its political difficulties by requiring further sacrifices (at least in the short run) from the population before Cuba can begin to make sustained economic progress. As such, these challenges are likely to intensify the political cleavages within Cuba.

As we noted above, Cuba's extensive social service programs were the linchpin in its social compact with its people. But the high costs of those programs (46 percent of its public expenditures in

1988) were unsustainable after the loss of Soviet economic assistance. The severe cutbacks in these programs after 1993 have contributed significantly to the impoverishment of the Cuban population, especially that of its pensioners, and to their growing disillusionment with the regime and the Revolution. Thus, restoring these social programs and increasing their real worth could provide an enormous boost to the new regime, as well as to the current regime.

But the aging of Cuba's population will make this task very difficult. We estimate that the growing numbers of elderly in the population (the fastest-growing cohorts will be those over 65) will increase pension expenditures by at least 50 percent, all else being equal. Moreover, these demographic pressures on Cuba's pension programs will be compounded by such pension-program features as the early ages of retirement, its pay-as-you-go funding, and the fact that public employees (the vast majority of all pensioners in Cuba) are not required to contribute to their retirement.

Indeed, even in the absence of the current economic crisis, the combination of these features of Cuba's pension system and the aging of its population would force the regime to alter its pension program. However, such policy alternatives as raising the qualifying age for pensions, reducing pension amounts, or forcing future retirees to pay for their retirement, are certain to generate political opposition and exacerbate the disillusionment with the regime.

Cuba's changing demographic structure will also raise issues about how much of its public resources it should devote to social expenditures and how much to investment, and how to allocate those social expenditures among different groups within the population. However, unlike most developed economies with aging populations, Cuba's low levels of income and economic development will make any decision to cut back current consumption in the interests of future economic growth particularly painful. Indeed, observers of Cuba's current economic predicament suggest that further cuts in consumption may be impossible and would produce adverse political fallout from those who depend most on government services. Maintaining social services, on the other hand, will increase the burden on Cuba's workers who have already absorbed cutbacks in real wages.

The allocation of social expenditures among the population is likely to be a complicated decision for at least two reasons. First, the increase in health and pension expenses will in all likelihood exceed the possible reductions in education expenditures from the decrease in Cuba's school-age population. Second, cutting back educational expenditures may be counterproductive, because Cuba's longer-term economic prospects are likely to depend upon the productivity (and thus the educational levels) of its labor force.

Cuba's demographic situation will also compound its economic difficulties, because within the next two decades it will very likely be facing a contraction in the size of its labor pool: The number of entrants into the labor pool will be smaller than the number leaving. If the Cuban government is to meet its future labor needs in the face of this demographic predicament, it will need to use its labor more efficiently and encourage higher labor-force participation among its population, and perhaps extend the traditional working years.[1] These changes, in turn, will require a reversal of two long-standing practices that have characterized the Cuban government's approach to employment: first, its policy of maintaining full-employment even when that translates (as it often has) into massive underemployment; and second, its policy of setting workers' wages according to a national pay schedule, rather than by their contribution to productivity, in an effort to minimize income differentials. Although reversing these policies may well encourage higher labor-force participation among the Cuban population, it would also increase income inequality.

An alternative for addressing this issue and one that some more-developed countries have considered would be to increase the size of the labor force by encouraging immigration. Return migration by Cuban-Americans, for example, could not only increase the size of the labor force but also add much-needed skills to the economy. However, it is difficult to imagine many Cuban-Americans (or others) choosing to migrate to Cuba (or their being encouraged to do so) under the current regime. Indeed, the most likely migration flow

---

[1] Cuban males currently qualify for state pensions at age 60; women, at age 55.

would seem to be in the opposite direction (Cubans leaving Cuba), which would, of course, compound the economy's labor problems.

As we have suggested, there are ways Cuba can deal with the demographic pressures it faces, but, in doing so, the Cuban government will be forced to choose to assign a higher priority to economic goals than to ideological goals—something it has heretofore been unwilling to do. Moreover, as other countries in a similar demographic position have discovered, these kinds of resource-allocation decisions necessarily revolve around questions of who wins and who loses and the priority to attach to the interests of different groups: workers versus retirees, the young versus the old, urban versus rural residents, Afro-Cubans versus whites. Although making these choices will resolve the allocation problem, it will also increase the political cleavages within the Cuban polity, thus compounding the political problems facing both the current and future Cuban governments.

Cuba's demographic situation is not the only structural challenge confronting the Cuban economy. Four and a half decades of central economic planning and three decades of tying Cuba's economic development to the Soviet Union and the Council for Mutual Economic Assistance have resulted in major institutional and structural obstacles to sustained economic growth.

Institutionally, Cuba's economy suffers from four major impediments: a labor force characterized by chronic low productivity, a small and deformed private sector, rampant corruption, and the absence of the rule of law. The Cuban government's employment policies, which have promoted underemployment and negated the incentive to work hard to reap the benefits of that labor, have resulted in a workforce with poor work habits, lack of on-the-job effort, and low productivity. As a result, an economy whose prospects will depend much more on the quality of its labor than on its quantity suffers from the paradox of a workforce with generally high levels of education but low productivity. Changing behaviors that are a by-product of decades of centralized planning will, as the experience of Eastern Europe has demonstrated, be painful and take longer than expected.

As the Eastern European experience also demonstrates, one way to expedite this change is to promote the growth of small and medium-sized enterprises to facilitate the transition from a centralized economy to a market economy. However, Cuban policies have severely constrained the development of a private sector and, despite the recent fitful efforts to legalize self-employment, have undermined the development of the entrepreneurial and the market skills necessary to build small businesses. Indeed, the Cuban government has actively discouraged the development of a wholesale market and impeded the growth of such occupations as managers, accountants, auditors, bankers, and insurers, which are central to the operation of a market economy. Instead, individuals who wish to take advantage of the limited opportunities for building small businesses have been forced to rely on the black market and other illegal practices to do so.

The onset of the Special Period has exacerbated the problem of corruption at both the individual and institutional levels in Cuba. Black markets, which tend to be endemic in centrally planned economies, exist in virtually all sectors of the Cuban economy. The supplies for these markets are, in turn, typically garnered by theft or misappropriation of government property. Corruption is also rampant at the governmental level, where officials indulge in influence-peddling, bribes, and exemptions from the rationing to which the public is subject in order to supplement their official salaries. The government's selective privatization of state enterprises has also emerged as a new form of public corruption for high-ranking members of the *nomenklatura.*

Reliance on the black market, corruption, and other illegal behavior appears to have become an essential element of the strategy Cubans rely on to survive the Special Period. Its net effect, however, is to impose a significant burden on the economy through the misallocation of public resources: It becomes an implicit tax that is appropriated by individuals rather than the state, and a penalty that must be paid by individuals who play by the rules of the game. Perhaps more important, these practices undermine the legitimacy of the state and increase public cynicism of the government and its programs.

Overcoming this legacy will require not just reducing the opportunities for corruption but changes in social attitudes and the development of institutions to promote transparency and accountability.

As the experience in Eastern Europe has again demonstrated, institutions such as a free press, the establishment of impartial and incorruptible legal and judicial institutions (hence the rule of law), and a civil society that not only expects but also demands such institutions, are central to reducing corruption. However, the type of political liberalization that is needed to support these changes has been an anathema to Castro and his regime: It threatens the regime's political dominance over Cuban society. A successor communist regime is likely to oppose such changes as well.

The final structural challenge facing Cuba is preparing its economy to enable it to compete in international markets. Although Cuba's economic fortunes rose or fell with the price of sugar on the world market even before the Revolution, the Castro regime's decision to tie the Cuban economy to the Soviet Union and the other CMEA states intensified the economy's dependence on sugar and left it unprepared to compete in world markets. Rather than diversifying its exports and building industries to serve its domestic market, Cuban economic planners responded to the extremely favorable prices paid by the CMEA for Cuban sugar (up to three times the international price) by concentrating its economic resources on sugar production. This development policy created an industrial structure depending too much on imported inputs, utilizing inefficient production techniques, relying too much on inferior Soviet technology, and lacking the industrial linkages necessary for the development of small-scale domestic suppliers.

Beginning in the early 1990s, the Cuban government has sought alternative sources for hard-currency exports in the tourist, nickel, and tobacco industries. But the economy still faces major restructuring problems. For example, the government has cut back sugar production and closed many sugar mills. Yet, it has been reluctant to lay off sugar workers or to allow foreign firms to invest much-needed capital in modernizing the industry. Moreover, much of Cuba's industrial and agricultural sectors was developed according to a CMEA model that relied heavily on vertically integrated production and imported inputs. Hence, Cuba will need to develop, from scratch, integrated supply chains that promote the development of small and medium-sized enterprises to facilitate a policy of import substitution. However, entrepreneurs (both foreign and domestic) will be reluctant to invest in such enterprises without the rule of law, which will protect their property rights, enforce contracts, and constrain the government from arbitrarily changing the rules of the game. Moreover, restructuring these industries will require both human and financial capital, which is currently in very short supply.

Rather than adopting policies that would help Cuba's economy make these adjustments, Castro has pursued a series of half-measures, more out of necessity than choice. The Cuban government, for example, has pursued foreign capital, but only on its own terms. It has closed sugar mills and cut back sugar production, but has also been reluctant to terminate the dislocated employees and perform the needed restructuring of the sugar industry. It has legalized self-employment but has placed substantial restrictions on the operations and profits of micro-enterprises. In sum, Castro's ideological and political imperatives have overridden economic imperatives for fundamental system change.

As this discussion has repeatedly noted, Cuba faces a formidable array of political and structural problems that will require wholesale political, social, institutional, and economic changes. But as we have also noted, Castro is unwilling to accept any changes that might challenge his complete primacy over decisionmaking in Cuba. However, the longer the Cuban government delays in dealing with these problems, the more difficult the eventual change is likely to be, the more politically disillusioned the public is likely to become with the regime, and the fewer degrees of freedom the government will have when it eventually takes action.

Implications for a Cuba After Castro

In light of Castro's intransigence, the challenge of confronting Cuba's myriad problems will in all likelihood fall to his successors. What domestic environment is that successor regime likely to face?

First, the government's recent imprisonment of Cuban dissidents and its obvious willingness to continue to repress any opposition has reduced the possibility of a democratic successor to Castro. Thus, at least in the short run, the successor regime is very likely to be drawn from Castro's inner circle and to be communist in ideology.

Second, with Fidel's departure, a communist successor regime will be forced to come to grips with the loss of the third traditional pillar that has supported the Cuban government in the past. As a result, it seems very likely that the major asset of a communist successor regime will be the one remaining pillar, the extensive state control apparatus.

Third, the strong probability that the successor regime will be drawn from the ranks of Fidel loyalists will make it less likely that the regime will be willing to undertake fundamental, systemic reform, and thus be able to solve Cuba's underlying economic problems. Hence, despite the fact that the reformers within the regime appear to have lost out in the short run, their prospects over the longer run could ultimately improve—especially if the military decides that it is in its best institutional interests to back the reformers to head off civil strife.

Fourth, the cleavages within Cuban society that have emerged during the Special Period are likely to intensify. Without solving the underlying structural problems facing the economy and restoring the social service structure, it seems very likely that the reemergence of racial disparities, the growing gap between the living standards of those who have access to the dollar economy and those who continue to be confined to the peso economy, and the growing disillusionment among the population with the Revolution, will all become worse. Indeed, to the extent that the successor regime attempts to deal with the demographic, institutional, and economic structural problems facing Cuba, the short-term result is very likely to be an increase in inequality, rising social tensions, and growing political discontent— particularly if the economy does not improve significantly for the majority of Cubans.

Fifth, the disaffection of Cuba's youth in particular and the depoliticization of the population in general, will make it more difficult for any successor regime (whether authoritarian or democratic) to gain the kind of support for the policies that are needed to confront Cuba's structural problems, since such policies are likely to be painful for at least some segments of the population. Also, judging by the Eastern European experience, the transition from the post-totalitarian Castro regime to a pluralist democratic state is likely to be messy (including the possibility of recrimination against informers and other members of the former regime) and to take a long time.

The international front also is likely to confront Castro's communist successors with an equally inhospitable environment. Since the collapse of communism worldwide, the Castro government's crackdown in spring 2003 has isolated Cuba as never before (Bond, 2003, p. 129):

> . . . [Castro's] actions sparked international anger that quickly hit Cuba where it hurt the most—in its economy. The governments that leapt to condemn his actions include some of his closest trading partners. Opponents of the embargo in the United States suddenly fell silent; embargo exemptions were not renewed; a U.S. agricultural fair in Havana was cancelled; and the European Union, after announcing that Cuba would qualify for extra European aid, hardened its "common position" still further.

Unless a democratic-transition occurs, or Castro's communist successors or the military embark on a new course by respecting human rights and opening up the polity and economy, Cuba's isolation is likely to continue after its *caudillo* is gone. Unless his heirs also abandon his hyper-nationalist postures toward Washington and now the EU, normalized diplomatic and trade relations with the United States will remain elusive, and ties with the EU would probably continue to be frozen. In turn, Cuba's prospects for obtaining economic assistance, credits, and investment capital from other international actors, such as the World Bank, International Monetary Fund, and Inter-American Development Bank, would be equally dim.

Given the internal and external challenges facing a successor regime, and the likelihood that an immediate successor communist regime will be unwilling or unable to introduce the reforms necessary to overcome those challenges, the Cuban Armed Forces are certain to play an important role in the post-Castro transition. How constructive the FAR's role will be remains to be seen, but it likely will be contingent not only on post-Castro succession dynamics at play within Cuba but also on U.S. policy and the actions of the Cuban-American community.

Policy Implications for the United States

It is beyond the scope of this study to discuss in detail the kind of policies the United States should pursue toward a post-Castro Cuba. Nevertheless, it is clear that whatever the United States does following Castro's demise is sure to be a major factor in whether Cuba remains under hard-line or reformist communist rule, falls under military governance, begins a democratic transition, or is gripped by political upheaval and recurrent instability. In this respect, some general policy guidelines can be extrapolated from the preceding analysis as a way of heading off the worst of these outcomes and helping steer post-Castro Cuba toward a new era that would benefit both the long-suffering Cuban people and the interests of the United States.

First, if the economic embargo is still in place, Washington should use the eventual lifting of that embargo as a major source of leverage to move a successor communist regime toward a democratic transition on the island. If a democratically oriented regime takes over, the embargo should be lifted immediately and followed by other steps, outlined below, to shore up the new government.

Second, work in concert with Canada and the United Kingdom, Spain, and other countries in the European Union in trying to influence the new post-Castro government to respect human rights, move toward a democratic transition, and liberalize the economy, and to help bolster the island's nascent civil-society forces.

Third, with respect to public diplomacy, the U.S. government should strive to avoid postures that will inflame Cuban nationalism and thus strengthen the hand of hard-liners in their struggle against reformers within the post-Castro regime, as well as against opponents outside the regime. Hence, cultivate military-to-military contacts and use public diplomacy to reassure other elites and the Cuban people that the United States will respect Cuba's independence, sovereignty, and dignity. However, the United States should also make clear that it will expect reciprocity in the new government taking steps toward realizing a democratic transition. At a minimum, that reciprocity should include scheduling free competitive elections, respecting human rights and pluralism, and opening up the economy along the lines of a free market.

Fourth, once the new Cuban government is committed to a democratic transition, the U.S. government should restore full diplomatic relations and two-way trade between the two countries, and offer economic and technical assistance to help jump-start the island's economy.

Fifth, the U.S. government should encourage the U.S. private sector, universities, NGOs, and, especially, the Cuban-American community, to actively engage a post-Castro Cuba that is embarked upon a democratic transition. These nongovernmental actors could be given tax and other incentives to promote trade and investment ties, establish academic exchanges and programs, and expand ties with Cuban NGOs. Cuban-Americans in particular can play a pivotal role in helping to revitalize the island's economy, not only by investing capital in new enterprises on the island but also by offering financial, technical, managerial, entrepreneurial, and legal assistance to both the new government and the newly emerging private sector.

Finally, when Cuba is at last on the path to a transition to democratic capitalism, the United States should offer to renegotiate the status of the Guantanamo Naval Base, perhaps along the lines of the 1977 Panama Canal treaties, thereby helping to infuse the new government with nationalist legitimacy.

The above steps may seem to commit the United States to promising too much to an island that has only 11.2 million inhabitants, no longer presents a serious security threat, and offers but modest trade and investment opportunities compared with a country like

China. Still, the United States cannot afford to neglect a Cuba after Castro, much less allow it to become a "failed state."

Cuba has always been of critical geostrategic importance to the United States because of its proximity and because it sits astride the principal sea-lanes of communication in the Caribbean. Today, the island's traditional geostrategic importance has been augmented by Cuba's potential for uncontrolled immigration, which could swamp Florida with hundreds of thousands, if not millions, of Cubans fleeing the island in the wake of the island's economic collapse and/or political strife. Even if immigration flows are checked, the United States could still be confronted with a humanitarian crisis on its doorstep. Moreover, the island offers a prime offshore location for drug-trafficking, which will become all the more prime if a new post-Castro government is corrupt and/or unable to govern effectively.

In the meantime, Castro's extraordinary, but mostly destructive, reign, thus far of more than 44 years, has demonstrated that the cost of ignoring Cuba has already been high, for both the Cuban people and the United States. Whatever accomplishments Cuba's "lord of misrule" has achieved have been accompanied by the island's impoverishment and his regime's anti-American animus and destabilizing activities in the hemisphere and elsewhere. Hence, when the great *caudillo* leaves the scene, Cuba will be at the crossroads of a new era—one that may lead toward continued economic crisis and repression, toward a political explosion, or toward a peaceful democratic transition. By offering Cuba a new deal such as that proposed above, the United States may increase the possibility that the Cuban people may ultimately be able to embark upon a constructive course that leads to a more prosperous, democratic future.

Bibliography

Bond, Theresa, "The Crackdown in Cuba," *Foreign Affairs,* Vol. 82, No. 5, September–October 2003. (Theresa Bond is a pseudonym for a political analyst specializing in closed societies.)

Casal, Lourdes, "Race Relations in Contemporary Cuba," in Philip Brenner, William M. Leo Grande, Donna Rich, and Daniel Siegel, eds., *The Cuban Reader: The Making of a Revolutionary Society,* New York: Grove Press, 1989.

Castro, Fidel, "Cuba Does Not Need the European Union to Survive and Develop," speech given on July 26, 2003; printed in *Digital Granma Internacional,* July 28, 2003.

Center for Cost and Financing Studies, *Medical Expenditure Panel Survey,* Washington, D.C.: Agency for Healthcare Research and Quality, 1996.

Central Intelligence Agency, *The World Factbook—Cuba,* 2002. Available at www.cia.gov/cia/publications/factbook.

Colas, Ramón, "Murder by Decree," Coral Gables, Fla.: University of Miami, Institute for Cuban and Cuban-American Studies, *Occasional Paper Series,* Issue 3, May 13, 2003.

Comisión Económica para América Latina y el Caribe, *La economía cubana: Reformas estructurales y desempeño en los noventa,* Mexico: Fondo de Cultura Económica, 1997.

Cuba News, February 2003, p. 5.

Cuba Transition Project, *Afro-Cubans Under the Castro Regime,* Staff Report, Coral Gables, Fla.: University of Miami, Issue 42, June 4, 2003a.

Cuba Transition Project, *Cuba's Economy in the Doldrums,* Staff Report, Coral Gables, Fla.: University of Miami, Institute for Cuban and Cuban-American Studies, Issue 43, June 18, 2003b.

Cuba Transition Project, *Repression Intensifying and Broadening in Cuba,* Staff Report, Coral Gables, Fla.: University of Miami, Institute for Cuban and Cuban-American Studies, Issue 41, April 30, 2003c.

Dahlburg, John-Thor, *Los Angeles Times,* July 25, 2003, p. A-15.

de la Fuente, Alejandro, "Recreating Racism: Race and Discrimination in Cuba's 'Special Period,'" Washington, D.C.: Georgetown University, Center for Latin American Studies, The Caribbean Project, *Cuba Briefing Paper,* No. 18, July 1998.

de la Torre, Miguel A., "Masking Hispanic Racism: A Cuban Case Study," *Journal of Hispanic/Latino Theology,* Vol. 6, No. 4, May 1999, pp. 57–74 (posted on the Afro-Cuba Web).

Domínguez, Jorge I., "Cuba's Elite Must Consider Life Without Castro," *The Miami Herald,* May 29, 2002 (posted by CubaNet on the Internet).

Domínguez, Jorge I., *Cuba: Order and Revolution,* Cambridge, Mass.: The Belknap Press of Harvard University Press, 1978.

Donate-Armada, Ricardo, "The Aging of the Cuban Population," in ASCE Staff, *Cuba in Transition,* Washington, D.C.: Association for the Study of the Cuban Economy (ASCE), 2001.

Economic Commission for Latin America and the Caribbean, *The Cuban Economy: Structural Reforms and Economic Performance in the 1990s,* New York: United Nations, December 2001.

Erikson, Daniel P., and Peter Wolf, "Cuba: What Next?" *Inter-American Dialogue: A Conference Report* (conference held in Washington, D.C., June 7, 2002), October 2002.

Espinosa, Juan Carlos, "Vanguard of the State: The Cuban Armed Forces in Transition, Problems of Communism," *Problems of Post-Communism,* November–December 2001.

Espinosa, Juan Carlos, and Robert C. Harding III, "Olive Green Parachutes and Slow Motion *Piñatas*: The Cuban Armed Forces in Comparative Perspective," paper presented at the conference "The Politics of Military Extrication in Comparative Perspective: Lessons for Cuba," Arrabida, Portugal, September 21–22, 2000.

Fernández, Damián J., "The Politics of Youth in Cuba: Patterns, Dynamics, and Future Challenges," in Edward Gonzalez and Kevin F. McCarthy, *Cuba After Castro: Legacies, Challenges, and Impediments: Appendices,* Appendix B, Santa Monica, Calif.: RAND Corporation, TR-131-RC, 2004.

Fernández, Damián J., *The Greatest Challenge: Civic Values in Post-Transition Cuba,* Coral Gables, Fla.: University of Miami, Institute for Cuban and Cuban-American Studies, Cuba Transition Project, 2003.

Fernández, Damián J., "Society, Civil Society, and the State—An Uneasy Three-Way Affair," *Problems of Post-Communism,* November–December 2001.

Foreign Broadcast Information Service, Latin America, December 12, 1991.

Gasperini, Lavinia, "The Cuban Educational System: Lessons and Dilemmas," Washington, D.C.: World Bank, *Country Study in Education Reform and Management Publication Series,* Vol. 1, No. 5, 2000.

Gayoso, "Transition in Central and Eastern Europe: Lessons for Development of SMEs in Cuba," in *Cuba in Transition,* Washington, D.C.: ASCE, 2000, pp. 72–76.

Gonzalez, David, "Cuban Dissident Says Castro Uses Invasion Fear as a Ploy," NYTimes.com, May 15, 2003.

Gonzalez, Edward, "The Legacies of Fidelismo and Totalitarianism," in Edward Gonzalez and Kevin F. McCarthy, *Cuba After Castro: Legacies, Challenges, and Impediments: Appendices,* Appendix A, Santa Monica, Calif.: RAND Corporation, TR-131-RC, 2004.

Gonzalez, Edward, *After Castro: Alternative Regimes and U.S. Policy,* Coral Gables, Fla.: University of Miami, Institute for Cuban and Cuban-American Studies, Cuba Transition Project, 2002a.

Gonzalez, Edward, *Ernesto's Ghost,* New Brunswick, N.J.: Transaction Publishers, 2002b.

Gonzalez, Edward, and Kevin F. McCarthy, *Cuba After Castro: Legacies, Challenges, and Impediments: Appendices,* Santa Monica, Calif.: RAND Corporation, TR-131-RC, 2004.

Gonzalez, Edward, and Tom S. Szayna, *Cuba and Lessons from Other Communist Transitions: A Workshop Report,* Santa Monica, Calif.: RAND Corporation, CF-142, 1998.

Gray, Cheryl W., and Daniel Kaufmann, "Corruption and Development," *Finance and Development,* March 1998, pp. 7–10.

Jatar-Hausmann, Ana Julia, *The Cuban Way: Capitalism, Communism, and Confrontation,* West Hartford, Conn.: Kumarian Press, 1999.

Henken, Ted, "A Taste of Capitalism: The Rise and Fall of Havana's Private Restaurants (*Paladares*)," paper presented at the meeting of the

Association for the Study of the Cuban Economy, Coral Gables, Fla., August 2002.

Hernandez-Cata, Ernesto, "The Fall and Recovery of the Cuban Economy in the 1990s: Mirage or Reality?" Washington, D.C.: International Monetary Fund (IMF), IMF Working Paper WP/01/48, 2000.

Kaufmann, Daniel, and Paul Siegelbaum, "Privatization and Corruption in Transition Economies," *Journal of International Affairs,* Vol. 50, No. 2, Winter 1997, pp. 80–94.

Klitgaard, Robert, *Controlling Corruption,* Berkeley, Calif.: University of California Press, 1988.

Latell, Brian, *The Cuban Military and Transition Dynamics,* Coral Gables, Fla.: University of Miami, Institute for Cuban and Cuban-American Studies, Cuba Transition Project, 2003.

Madrid-Aris, Manuel, "Education's Contribution to Economic Growth in Cuba," in ASCE Staff, *Cuba in Transition,* Washington, D.C.: ASCE, 2000.

Márquez Linares, Claudia (Grupo Decoro), "Racismo institucionalizado," *CubaNet Independiente,* December 20, 2002.

Massetti, Jorge, *In the Pirate's Den—My Life as a Secret Agent for Castro,* San Francisco, Calif.: Encounter Books, 2003.

Mauro, Paolo, "The Effects of Corruption on Growth, Investment, and Government Expenditure: A Cross-Country Analysis," in Kimberley Ann Elliott, ed., *Corruption and the Global Economy,* Washington, D.C.: Institute for International Economics, 1997, pp. 83–108.

Mauro, Paolo, "Corruption and Growth," *Quarterly Journal of Economics,* Vol. 110, 1995, pp. 681–712.

McCarthy, Kevin F., "Cuba's Demographic Future and Its Implications," in Edward Gonzalez and Kevin F. McCarthy, *Cuba After Castro: Legacies, Challenges, and Impediments: Appendices,* Appendix C, Santa Monica, Calif.: RAND Corporation, TR-131-RC, 2004.

Mesa-Lago, Carmelo, *Growing Economic and Social Disparities in Cuba: Impact and Recommendations for Change,* Coral Gables, Fla.: University of Miami, Institute for Cuban and Cuban-American Studies, Cuba Transition Project, 2003a.

Mesa-Lago, Carmelo, "The Slowdown of the Cuban Economy in 2001–2002: External Causes or Domestic Malaise?" Coral Gables, Fla.: University of Miami, Institute for Cuban and Cuban-American Studies, *Occasional Paper Series,* March 2003b.

Mesa-Lago, Carmelo, *Growing Economic and Social Disparities in Cuba,* Coral Gables, Fla.: University of Miami, Institute for Cuban and Cuban-American Studies, 2002.

Mesa-Lago, Carmelo, "The Cuban Economy in 1999–2001: Evaluation of Performance and Debate on the Future," in ASCE Staff, *Cuba in Transition,* Washington, D.C.: ASCE, 2001.

Mesa-Lago, Carmelo, *Market, Socialist and Mixed Economies: Comparative Policy and Performance—Chile, Cuba, and Costa Rica,* Baltimore, Md.: The Johns Hopkins University Press, 2000.

Montejo, Estéban, *The Autobiography of a Runaway Slave,* Miguel Barnet, ed., Jocasta Innes, transl., New York: Pantheon Books, 1968.

Moore, Carlos (Center for Latin American Studies, UCLA), *Castro, the Blacks, and Africa,* Berkeley, Calif.: University of California Press, 1988.

New York Times, May 18, 2003, p. 10.

Oficina Nacional de Estadísticas (ONE), *Anuario estadístico de Cuba 2000,* La Habana, 2001.

Patallo Sánchez, Laura, *Establishing the Rule of Law in Cuba,* Coral Gables, Fla.: University of Miami, Institute for Cuban and Cuban-American Studies, Cuba Transition Project, 2003.

Pérez, Lorenzo L., "The Pension System of Cuba: The Current Situation and Implications of International Pension Reform Experiences for Addressing Cuba's Problems," in Association for the Study of the Cuban Economy, *Cuba in Transition,* Volume 8, Washington, D.C.: ASCE, 1998, pp. 520–534.

Pérez, Louis A., Jr., *Cuba: Between Reform and Revolution,* New York: Oxford University Press, 1988.

Pérez-López, Jorge F., "The Legacies of Socialism: Some Implications for the Cuban Transition," in Edward Gonzalez and Kevin F. McCarthy, *Cuba After Castro: Legacies, Challenges, and Impediments: Appendices,* Appendix D, Santa Monica, Calif.: RAND Corporation, TR-131-RC, 2004a.

Pérez-López, Jorge F., "The Cuban Sugar Industry After the Transition," in Edward Gonzalez and Kevin F. McCarthy, *Cuba After Castro: Legacies, Challenges, and Impediments: Appendices,* Appendix E, Santa Monica, Calif.: RAND Corporation, TR-131-RC, 2004b.

Pérez-López, Jorge, "Waiting for Godot: Cuba's Stalled Reforms and Continuing Economic Crisis," *Problems of Post-Communism,* November–December 2001, pp. 44–45.

"Preocupa a Comunistas Jóvenes la repression en Cuba," *Contacto Magazine,* from ContactoNews@aol.com, April 15, 2003.

Reporters Without Borders, "Cuba: One Hundred Days of Solitude," press release, Paris, June 24, 2003a.

Reporters Without Borders, *Cuba: The State of Press Freedom,* Paris: Reporters Without Borders, June 24, 2003b.

Revolución, March 13, 1959, p. 11.

Rodríguez, José Luis, *Estrategia del desarrollo economico en Cuba,* La Habana: Editorial de Ciencias Sociales, 1990.

Romero, Simon, "Cuban Music Star Defects to U.S. with Entourage," nytimes.com, June 11, 2003.

Sawyer, Mark Q., "Race and the Future of Cuba," Los Angeles, Calif.: UCLA, unpublished manuscript, paper prepared for RAND, 2002.

Suchlicki, Jaime, ed., *The Cuban Military Under Castro,* Coral Gables, Fla.: University of Miami, Graduate School of International Studies, Inter-American Studies, 1989.

Tattlin, Isadora, *Cuban Diaries: An American Housewife in Havana,* Chapel Hill, N.C.: Algonquin Books of Chapel Hill, 2002.

Williams, Carol J., "Cubans Find Tourism Is the Best Way to Make a Buck," *Los Angeles Times,* September 6, 2003, p. A-3.

World Bank, "The Fight Against Corruption: A World Bank Perspective," Consultive Group Meeting for the Reconstruction and Transformation of Central America, Stockholm, 1999.

Zeitlin, Maurice, *Revolutionary Politics and the Cuban Working Class,* New York: Harper Torchbooks, 1970.